# Jesus
# ONLY

# Jesus ONLY

## VANCE HAVNER

Kingsley Press

Shoals, Indiana

*Jesus Only*

Published by Kingsley Press
PO Box 973
Shoals, IN 47581
USA

Tel. (800) 971-7985
www.kingsleypress.com
E-mail: sales@kingsleypress.com

ISBN: 978-1-937428-60-0

First Kingsley Press edition 2016

This first Kingsley Press edition is published under license from Baker Publishing Group.

# Contents

# Preface

During the years since *Jesus Only* has been out of print I have had so many requests and inquiries about it that we are reactivating it with several additional messages not published heretofore. In the awful confusion of these tragic days many dear souls are weary of the torrent of words to no profit—stacks of books by blind leaders of the blind and panaceas from experts who do not know what the question is, much less the answer. They long to press through the throng to Christ himself and touch him for themselves. It is our hope and prayer that these meditations may help any and all who would see no man, but Jesus only.

*—Vance Havner*

# CHAPTER 1

# Jesus Only

I would like to begin with a personal testimony. My own spiritual experience has gone through three stages. I was converted at the age of ten. The next year I became a preacher, and for some years thereafter I preached a simple gospel message.

Later I moved into a more liberal position. It was during those halcyon days just after the first World War. Dreams of world peace and human brotherhood were challenging youthful enthusiasm. Certain modernist preachers were becoming popular and their new approach seemed to set forth the old wine in new bottles. It was evident to me later that the old wine was thrown out with the old bottles but I had not discovered that as yet. I felt that the time had come to strike out on new trails for higher altitudes and so I began to preach about the "new position" and "outmoded categories."

But the trail of the modern mind, left to itself, runs out in the wilderness, and blessed is the man who wakes up in time to see how he is being deceived by these peddlers of new light. From this muddle the Lord delivered me. My first reaction was to plunge into a very stern fundamentalism. I fear that I was rather like the Scotsman who said he was open to conviction but would like to see the man who could convict him! There was a tendency to call down fire on the Samaritans and an inclination to forget what manner of spirit I was of.

For years now I have moved around among many grades and shades and varieties of conservative Christians, preaching in churches and conferences. Such a ministry ranges from staid old churches to popular gospel tabernacles. In some places I have almost frozen, spiritually, and in others I have almost fried. I have listened to many voices, some well-known and many unknown, analyzing the situation and prescribing the remedy. I have tried to move among all groups, belonging to as few as possible in order that I might be the servant of all. It has been and still is a rich and rewarding experience, for in this day of apostasy there are many precious souls all over the land who fear the Lord and speak often one to another. They have many faults and failings, but I had rather take Bible Christians at their worst than this world at its best. I bless God for the tie that binds our hearts in Christian love.

Out of all this I have come to a fixed conclusion: the issue is simply Jesus Christ. Spurgeon said: "In the days of Paul the sum and substance of theology was Jesus Christ. I am not ashamed to avow myself a Calvinist. I do not hesitate to take the name of Baptist. But if you ask what is my creed, I must answer: it is Jesus Christ." One thinks of A. B. Simpson's early years of seeking this experience and that, culminating in the conclusion so well stated in his poem, beginning,

Once it was the blessing,
Now it is the Lord.

How we like to make a Santa Claus of the Lord, seeking only his gifts! Happy are we when we seek the Giver rather than the gift and can both sing and pray:

Now thee alone I seek,
Give what is best.

My message therefore is simply Jesus Christ. He is enough. Of course we are familiar with the fact that Christ is the Christian's life and message, but we need to familiarize ourselves with the familiar. We assume what we ought to assert. He is the hub, but too many of us are out on our favorite spokes like owls on different limbs. When we stand at the hub all the spokes are ours. And the closer we are to the hub the closer we are to all the spokes!

Of course, I do not mean the Christ of partyism. Some say, "I belong to Christ," just in order to dodge issues. There was a Christ-party in Corinth along with the Paul-party, the Cephas-party, and the Apollos-party. And they were as bad as the others and maybe a little worse! Christ does not exclude Paul and Cephas and Apollos, he includes them. All the gospel preachers are ours because we are Christ's. The only thing that is not ours is us; we are not our own, we are bought with a price.

Certainly I do not mean the Christ of modernism. That is a false Christ. My Christ is the virgin-born Son of God who lived a sinless life, died a substitutionary, atoning death, rose bodily from the grave, and is coming again to reign.

Some years ago, while preaching in a small Southern town, I was walking around one afternoon meditating on the evening message. I became impressed that I needed to preach "Jesus Only" more than I had been doing. I remember that I asked the Lord to confirm that impression by giving me one soul that night. Evening came and I preached. I gave the invitation but no one responded. As I pronounced the benediction, I thought, "Lord, where is the soul I asked for?" Before the "amen" was reached a downpour of rain set in, so that the people could not get home. A man came to me and asked that we might pray together. We went to a small room and there he received Christ as his Savior. I have thought of that incident many times since and have tried to be true to the impression it confirmed.

There is only one safe and sure center of Christian experience, doctrine, and testimony and that is Jesus Christ. Stand at any other point, no matter how good, and you will become lopsided. Stand with him and you keep your balance, for by him all things consist.

# CHAPTER 2

# By Him All Things Consist

When Paul declared in Ephesians that "Christ filleth all in all" and in Colossians that "Christ is all and in all," he was not merely giving us pious phrases to roll under our tongues; he was stating the fixed and fundamental fact of the allness of Jesus Christ. Christ was everything to Paul. To the Corinthians he had written, "I determined not to know anything among you save Jesus Christ and him crucified." To the Galatians he wrote: "God forbid that I should glory save in the cross of the Lord Jesus Christ." To the Ephesians he wrote of him who "filleth all in all," and to the Philippians he declared, "To me to live is Christ."

Writing to the Colossians, he met an outbreak of heresy not so much by pointing out its errors, although he did that, as by presenting the Lord Jesus Christ as "the image of the invisible God," "Christ in you, the hope of glory," "in whom are hid all the treasures of wisdom and knowledge," "Christ, who is our life," "Christ, all and in all."

It has been a long time since Colossians was written, but there is the same tendency to belittle our Lord. Thousands of Christians localize him in their thinking either to Palestine a long time ago or at the Father's right hand now. One thinks of the preacher, back from a trip to the Holy Land, who bored everybody by continually relating it. Finally, an old preacher observed, "I'd rather walk with Christ five minutes now than five years where he has been!" We need the sweep of Paul's vision to see Christ past, present, and future. No wonder so many Christians are pale, sickly, anemic: they do not know what a Christ they have. If Jesus is the Alpha and Omega, Beginning and Ending,

Author and Finisher of our faith, if by him all things consist, it follows that everything centers and converges in him.

By him creation consists. "For by him were all things created that are in heaven and that are in earth, visible and invisible, whether they be thrones or dominions or principalities or powers; all things were created by him and for him" (Col. 1:16). How many Christians ever think of Christ as the one "by whom all things are created," as Colossians puts it; "by whom all things were made" as John puts it; "by whom God made the worlds," as Hebrews put it? Why did God make the universe, anyway? He made it that one day Christ might be all in all, that one day, from tiniest electron to mightiest planet, it might glorify Jesus. Scientists cannot give the reason for the universe: Christ is the reason. Creation is now enslaved in corruption, but one day it will display the glory of Christ, the bondage of sin will be broken, the sons of God be manifested. And Christ not only created the universe and is its object but he sustains it now. The very existence of each of us, to say nothing of our salvation, depends on him. Without him the universe would fall apart.

By him redemption consists. In order to conform men to the image of his Son, God gave his Son. There is no salvation in any other.

By him the gospel consists. The gospel is simply the good news about Jesus, that he came, died, and rose again. It is not a program, plan, or philosophy that saves, but a person. It takes a person to reach persons, a life to reach lives. The gospel is a personal matter: "HE shall save his people from THEIR sins." "I if I be lifted up will draw all men unto ME."

By him the Bible consists. True, we see Christ in the light of the Scriptures, for they are they which testify of him. But we can see the Scriptures only in the light of Christ. He is the key to the Scriptures. He expounded unto his disciples in all the Scriptures the things concerning HIMSELF. All roads lead to him throughout the Book. Someone has said that the Pentateuch gives us the foreshadowings of Christ; the prophets, the foretellings of Christ; the Psalms, the feelings of Christ; the Gospels, the facts of Christ; the epistles, the fruits of Christ.

By him the church consists. "God gave him to be head over all things to the church, which is his body, the fulness of him that filleth all in all" (Eph. 1:22-23). We are married to him, members of his body. Any group that feeds on itself and not on Christ is a monstrosity, for it is a headless body.

By him doctrine consists. Some Christians become disciples of a phrase instead of a person, they harp on one string and ride one hobby. Some get off on a tangent on sanctification, for instance. But sanctification, strictly speaking, is not just a doctrine: Christ is our sanctification (1 Cor. 1:30). Spurgeon said, "Holiness is not the way to Christ; Christ is the way to holiness." Better still, Christ is our holiness.

Some make the Holy Spirit the figurehead of movements, but the Spirit testifies not of himself but of Christ (John 15:26). In that classic passage on the Spirit, John 7:37-39, it is Jesus who is at the center of the stage: "If any man thirst, let him come unto ME and drink. He that believeth on ME, as the Scripture hath said, from within him shall flow rivers of living water. This spake HE of the Spirit which they that believe on HIM should receive: for the Holy Ghost was not yet given; because that JESUS was not yet glorified." Any supposed experience of the Spirit that draws attention to itself and not to Christ is not to be trusted.

By him the resurrection consists. Jesus said to Martha, "Thy brother shall rise again." She said, "I know that he shall rise again in the resurrection at the last day." Martha was orthodox, but she needed to move from the doctrinal to the personal. So Jesus said, "I am the resurrection and the life." The resurrection is not something to believe but someone to believe.

By him faith consists. It is not the quantity or the quality but the object of our faith that matters. Saving faith is faith in Christ, not merely believing things about Christ. The man with best nerves is the man least conscious of his nerves; and the man with best faith is the man least conscious of his faith but most conscious of his Christ.

By him all Christian experience consists. The Christian life is simply Christ, the indwelling and outliving Christ. "To me to live is Christ." The victorious life or the abundant or deeper life, whatever you choose to call it, is just Christ, more of Christ and less of self. He is our life, not just a teacher of how to live.

By him separation consists. He is the great divider, who came not to send peace but a sword, and he must separate us. Separation is not just quitting things, it is going unto HIM without the camp bearing HIS reproach. When he was on earth there was often a division of the people on account of him, and he still divides men today. But there are also those who cause division among us; they are to be watched and avoided.

The main thing about the Lord's return is the Lord. Some are looking merely for something to happen, not for someone to come. We are not looking for a program of events but for a person.

By him Christian fellowship consists. "Our fellowship is with the Father, and with his Son Jesus Christ" (1 John 1:3). I have heard of a church with a "Jesus Only" sign in front. One night a storm blew out the first three letters and left "Us Only." That has happened in more ways than one these days. The basis of fellowship is Jesus Christ. You cannot get the saints together at any other point. We are already one in him. We have so many cliques now that an appropriate greeting would be, "How are you clique-ing?" Some saints have no testimony, only an argument. The mark of true fellowship is "love to all the saints," which springs from "faith in Christ Jesus" (Col. 1:4).

Indeed by him testimony consists. We are his witnesses, not his lawyers. "We preach not ourselves but Christ Jesus the Lord." There is too much sermonizing and too little witnessing. People do not come to Christ at the end of an argument. Simon Peter comes to Jesus because Andrew goes after him with a testimony.

By him our fruitfulness consists. "He that abideth in me and I in him, the same bringeth forth much fruit: for without me ye can do nothing" (John 15:5). It is not what is done for him but by him that counts. I wonder how much of our church activity really proceeds from him. We think it depends on us, our effort, our organization, our enthusiasm. We need to get our eyes off our efficiency and on his sufficiency.

By him the answer to every need consists. God has promised to supply all our need according to his riches in glory by Christ Jesus. If we need victory, we can reign in life through Christ Jesus. If we need peace, the peace of God will garrison our hearts through Christ Jesus. If we need wisdom, he is our wisdom. If we need strength, we can do all things through Christ. Like the hungry multitude of old, we need not depart from him for anything.

By him the future consists. For the believer, the prospect is not merely going to heaven but departing to be WITH CHRIST. It is his presence that makes heaven so glorious. And it is separation from him that is hell's worst feature. It is all the difference between "Come, ye blessed of my Father" and "Depart, I never knew you." To be cut off from him who is life cannot but be unending death; to be cut off from the Light can be but eternal darkness. The most glorious thing about heaven is that we shall be like HIM.

By him the future of the universe created by him and consisting by him will be consummated in him. In the dispensation of the fulness of times God will gather together in one all things in Christ, in heaven, and on earth, even in him.

The little girl who, failing to reassemble a torn-up map of the United States, discovered that on the reverse side was a picture of George Washington and that by putting his picture together she also assembled the map, illustrates a profounder truth. Nothing can be assembled, either one's life or the universe, apart from Christ. But when we know him all things else find their place, for by him all things consist, and we are complete in him.

CHAPTER 3

# What Christit Means To Me

It is a privilege to speak to my friends in the name of him who has called us his friends if we do the things which he commands us. Someone asked Charles Kingsley, "What is the secret of your beautiful life?" He answered, "I had a friend." And I have often thought that if this life of mine ever approaches the beautiful and true it will be because

> I've found a friend, O such a friend!
> He loved me ere I knew him;
> He drew me with the cords of love,
> And thus he bound me to him.

There are many things about which I am too ignorant to speak wisely—and, I hope, too wise to speak ignorantly—but I can speak of Christ with freedom, for then I am boasting of another and not of myself. Josh Billings used to say, "I'd rather know a few things for certain than be sure of a lot of things that ain't so!" In a day when men are chasing a thousand and one things that "ain't so" I rejoice in "Jesus Christ the same."

I have found in Christ a life that is beautifully simple and simply beautiful. In him I find, first of all, PARDON. "God for Christ's sake hath forgiven you." I have read of a Russian soldier who, years ago, sat in his tent one night before a list of debts he could not pay. He had written at the bottom of the list, "Who is to pay for all this?" As the hours went by, he finally fell asleep. The emperor came by, looked in the tent, saw the soldier, came up closer, saw the list of debts and the pitiful question. It is said that the emperor affixed his own royal signature to the bottom of

19

the list, so that when the soldier awoke, he found his debts paid. I know that once I faced moral and spiritual debts which I could not pay. But Jesus, with the blood of Calvary, wrote, "Son, thy sins be forgiven thee." Is it any wonder that rainy days become radiant days when the heart can sing?

> Jesus paid it all;
> All to him I owe.
> Sin had left a crimson stain;
> He washed it white as snow.

Because Christ means pardon, he also means PEACE to me. Through him I have peace with God; and as I make my requests known to God with thanksgiving, the peace of God which passes all understanding—and all misunderstanding too!—garrisons my heart and mind through Christ Jesus. This world has no peace: "There is no peace, saith the Lord, unto the wicked." We are all so crazy these days that it has been reported that monkeys have been known to go insane watching people on the outside of their cages! Someone has spelled modern life in three words, "Hurry, Worry, Bury." The world has insomnia of the soul. It has tried all the opiates and sedatives, but there is only one prophylactic against fear and worry. You don't keep it, it keeps you: "My peace I give unto you, not as the world giveth."

Then Christ gives me a PURPOSE: "To live is Christ." An irate woman met her husband when he got off a merry-go-round and said, "Now, look at you: you spent your money, you got off right where you got on, and you ain't been nowhere!" It is a perfect picture of modern living. An African-American philosopher once said, "One reason why some folks never git nowhar is, they wa'n't gwine nowhar when they started." But Christ gives us a purpose, and that purpose is just himself. As the Mississippi flows through the middle of America and the tributaries feed into it on both sides, so when one seeks first the kingdom of God and his righteousness, all else flows into that central purpose, to know Christ and to make him known.

Christ also means POWER, the power to see the purpose through. "All power is given unto me," he said, and Paul declares, "I can do all things through Christ." Jesus is not only our Savior, he is our sustenance; he is "the power of God." His power is made real to us by the Holy Spirit, not that we may brag about it but that we may be his witnesses.

And then he means PLENTY, spiritual abundance. "All things are yours," says Paul to the Christian. Again he speaks of "having nothing, yet possessing all things." It is the Christian's paradox. He doesn't have to get rich, he is rich, for "the Lord is rich unto all that call upon him." Most of us appreciate but do not appropriate what we have in Christ. We carry checks on the bank of heaven and never cash them at the window of prayer. We are Bible window-shoppers: we stroll up and down through the show-windows of God's Word and never possess what we perceive. God, who spared not Hhis Son, shall with him also freely give us all things.

Finally, Christ gives me an eternal PROSPECT. "Where I am, there ye may be also." Someone has said, with reference to the life to come, that in the Old Testament they were willing to go but wanting to stay, while in the New they were wanting to go but willing to stay. Jesus had made the difference. And what a difference it makes to be with Christ! A mother whose little son had died, told her little daughter, "Your brother has gone to be with Jesus." Later, in conversation with a friend, she spoke of having lost her little boy. The daughter spoke up and said, "But, mother, you said he was with Jesus. How can he be lost if you know where he is!" Truly, the Christian can say of his departed loved ones in Christ:

> Death can hide but not divide;
> Thou art but on Christ's other side.
> Thou art with Christ and Christ with me;
> In Christ united still are we.

These are some things Christ means to me. All I need is found in him. He is Alpha and Omega and all the letters between. He is the same yesterday, the historic Christ; the same today, the indwelling Christ; the same tomorrow, the coming Christ.

People ask me sometimes, What is your persuasion? I tell them that I am of Paul's persuasion: persuaded that nothing can separate me from God's love in Christ; persuaded that he is able to keep what I have committed against that day; and, knowing the terror of the Lord, constrained by the love of Christ, I would persuade men.

Christ is my message. Some years ago, two boats were passing each other on the Mississippi, when an old African-American said to a white passenger as he pointed to the other boat, "Look, yonder's the captain!" When asked for an explanation, he said, "Years ago, we were goin' along like this and I fell overboard and the captain rescued me. And since then, I just loves to point him out!"

Some years ago, this writer was overboard, in water too deep for his wit and will to navigate. But the Captain of our salvation leaped overboard from glory to rescue him. And I just love to point him out!

# CHAPTER 4

# Gathering With Christ

*"He that is not with me is against me; and he that gathereth not with me scattereth abroad" (Matthew 12:30).*

W e are living in a day of hazy standards of right and wrong. The old line of demarcation has practically disappeared from modern thinking. A prominent minister said: "The delineation of sin has undergone a transformation somewhat similar to that which has taken place in the world of painting. The old clearcut lines have given way to an impressionistic indefiniteness, the black and white contrasts to low-toned grays. The churches have adopted a hush policy on the doctrine of depravity and a rotarian gospel takes the place of repentance."

I like his reference to painting. There was a time when you could look at a picture and tell what it was. Today black and white have become gray. Someone has said: "The religion of China is Confucian; the religion of America is confusion." A country schoolteacher, applying for a job, was asked, "Do you teach that the earth is round or flat?" "Which way do you want it taught?" was the reply. "I can teach it either way." Something like that is the attitude of many a pulpit today.

A late university president said, "We need a reaffirmation, not only in thought but in practice, of the fundamental distinction between right and wrong." And a leading American philosopher has written: "One trouble with America is, our people have lost a clear conviction as to what is right and what is wrong."

The Lord Jesus had no vague notions along this line. To him evil was not imperfect goodness. It has been said that we divide the human race horizontally, high class, middle class, low class;

but Christ divided it perpendicularly, to the right and to the left. He does just that in our text.

Furthermore, he declares himself to be the great Gatherer. He is the Gatherer of Israel. In Psalm 106:47 we read, "Save us, O Lord, and gather us from among the heathen." In Isaiah 11:12 it is said that God "shall gather together the dispersed of Judah from the four corners of the earth." He promises, "I will gather you from all nations" (Jer. 29:14). Again, "I will even gather you from the people, and assemble you out of the countries where ye have been scattered, and I will give you the land of Israel" (Ezek. 11:17).

Our Lord came first to the lost sheep of the house of Israel. He came unto his own and his own received him not, and he said, "How often would I have gathered thy children together, even as a hen gathereth her chickens under his wings, and ye would not" (Matt. 23:37). Today he is gathering individual Jews as well as Gentiles; but one day there will be a national gathering of Israel, for God has promised it.

Then he is the Gatherer of Gentiles during this age, while Israel, nationally, is set aside. When Israel refused him, he turned as a light to the Gentiles. In the Acts you find the apostles turning to the Gentiles with the gospel which is the power of God unto salvation, to the Jew first and also to the Greek.

Even Caiaphas, the high priest, prophesied that Jesus should "gather together in one the children of God that were scattered abroad" (John 11:52).

He is the Gatherer of the church, the Ecclesia, the out-called ones. God is not converting the world but taking out a people for his name (Acts 15:14).

One day our Lord will gather up the saints when he gathers the wheat into the barn (Matt. 13:30) at the rapture of the believers (1 Thess. 4:13-18). "He shall send his angels with a great sound of a trumpet, and they shall gather together his elect from the four winds, from one end of heaven to the other" (Matt. 24:31).

There will not only be an up-gathering but also an out-gathering when "the Son of Man shall send forth his angels, and they shall gather out of his kingdom all things that offend, and them which do iniquity; and shall cast them into a furnace of fire: there shall be wailing and gnashing of teeth" (Matt. 13:41,42).

Finally, we are told of God's purpose "that in the dispensation of the fulness of times he might gather together in one all things in Christ, both which are in heaven, and which are on earth; even in him" (Eph. 1:10).

What do we have in all these verses and many more like them? We have Christ, the rejected Gatherer of Israel; Christ, the Gatherer of Gentiles; Christ, the Gatherer of the church; Christ, the Up-Gatherer of the saints; Christ, the Out-Gatherer of all that offends; Christ, the Gatherer of all things in himself. Now, look at our text again: "He that gathereth not with me scattereth abroad."

It is obvious that Christ is the center of unity. "By him all things consist" (Col. 1:17). A Christian is eccentric because he revolves around a different center. I do not mean that he has to be queer, let his hair grow long, wear a robe and sandals, and carry a walking stick. He is eccentric because Christ is the center of his life, whereas most people revolve around some other center.

We have never heard more about unity and had less of it than in the past few years. When the first disarmament conference was held in London, Will Rogers said, "Those fellows might get somewhere if it wasn't for human nature." He spoke well, for you cannot get humanity together so it will stay together, except in Christ. There is no other force that will hold them. Organization will not hold them; they unite only in the body of Christ. Babel was man's effort at unity, and God cursed it with tongues nobody could understand; Pentecost was God's plan of unity and he blessed it with tongues everybody could understand. We have denominational differences, to be sure; but I am not speaking of unanimity or of unification but of unity, the unity of the Spirit.

Now, Christ is the great Gatherer, and if we do not gather with him he makes it plain that we scatter, we work against him. The only way we can help him gather is by winning souls and fishing for men. Mind you, if we are not engaged in some form of this great gathering, we are not merely indifferent; we are not neutral. He made it plain that we are instruments of division and discord, that if we are not active with him we are active against him. No matter how much you may wave a Bible, if you are not gathering with Christ you are not merely wasting time, you are working against the only unifying force in all existence.

But we cannot gather with Christ if we are not first with him: "He that is not WITH me is against me." The believer's position is stated first, then his practice, gathering with Christ: first, doctrine, then duty. Salvation and service are set here in their correct order. We are with him in the heavenlies, gathering with him in the earthlies. "Dead with Christ," "crucified with Christ," "risen with Christ," "quickened together with Christ," "hid with Christ," "joint-heirs with Christ," "reign with Christ"; such is our blessed position. And we are not here to work for him but with him.

To sum it up, anyone who is not with Christ in redemption, regeneration, sanctification, and who is not engaged in winning others to him is against Christ. He may be working for world peace, civic improvement, social justice, the art clubs, the cultured set, "Who's Who" and What's What, every branch and band of the Amalgamated Sons of Old Adam; but if he is not identified with Christ in position and practice he is anti-Christ.

This terrific text recognizes only two classes. A radio preacher has objected to classifying the human race as saints and sinners, lost and saved. But it is Christ who does the classifying, and here with the sharp two-edged sword of his Word he splits mankind asunder and the issue is our relationship to him. He did not even say, "He that gathereth not with a church." This leaves some church workers out in the cold and lets a lot of religious activity go by the board. There are well-meaning folk who labor adding names to rolls, proselyting right and left for class or league or union, trying to tantalize the world into the church with a rummage sale, handing out dishes of hot water with one lonesome oyster chasing around as if seeking a lost companion, gathering for a church but unwilling to cross the street to gather to Christ.

You will remember that when Jesus commanded the disciples to launch out into the deep and let down their nets, Peter said, "Master, we have toiled all the night and have taken nothing." Anything that starts with "we" always ends with "nothing" when Christ is not in the boat! But Peter went on to say, "Nevertheless, at thy word, I will let down the net." I like to think of "nevertheless" as a bridge over which Peter crosses to put Christ first: "At THY word, I will...." After that, things began to happen and the fish were hauled in. And when Peter besought the Lord to depart, Jesus answered, "Fear not; from henceforth thou shalt catch men." And he certainly caught some on the day of Pentecost!

Are you trying to gather with Christ in your own strength? Have you toiled and taken nothing? Put him first: "At THY word I will...." And "from henceforth thou shalt catch men," for he has said, "Follow me and I WILL MAKE YOU fishers of men."

# CHAPTER 5

# The Forgotten Beatitude

*"Blessed is he, whosoever shall not be offended in me"(Matthew 11:6).*

We are familiar with the beatitudes of the Sermon on the Mount. We are also acquainted with other beatitudes of our Lord, such as, "Blessed is that servant whom his Lord when he cometh shall find so doing"; "Blessed are they that hear the word of God and keep it."

But here is a little beatitude, short and sandwiched between longer verses, so that we are in danger of passing it up altogether.

John the Baptist was in prison. That rugged, ascetic Elijah of the New Testament, prophet of the outdoors, was certainly out of place in a damp, dark dungeon. No wonder he had the blues. One day his feelings hit a record low and he sent a delegation to Jesus to ask, "Art thou he that should come or do we look for another?" Now, that was a serious doubt for John the Baptist. The very thing he had preached like a living exclamation point had become a question mark to the preacher himself. It was not the first or last time that a preacher's affirmation has become, in a dungeon, a preacher's interrogation. It reminds us of another prophet of the dungeon, Jeremiah, who cried to God from the depths, "Wilt thou be altogether unto me as a liar and as waters that fail?"

But our Lord did not reprimand John the Baptist. It is noteworthy that two of the strongest characters in the Bible had something akin to a nervous breakdown. Elijah, in the Old Testament, collapsed under the juniper, and God had to feed and rest him. More than one Christian, exhausted, with nerves on edge, has imagined that he is the last survivor of the saints. And usually he needs not reproof but rest. Then here is John the Baptist of the camel's hair vestments and victuals of locusts and wild honey, who could reprove kings and call religious people sons of snakes; here is John the Baptist down in the dumps even as you and I! It is one thing to stand on Jordan and give it, another thing to stay in jail and take it!

But what did Jesus do? Did he bitterly reprove the troubled prophet? Did he say, "I'm ashamed of you, disappointed in you. What will people think?" He did nothing of the sort. He did not even send John a tract on "How To Be Happy In Jail!" On the contrary, on the day that John the Baptist made his poorest remark about Jesus, Jesus said the best thing about John the Baptist: "Among them that are born of women there hath not risen a greater than John the Baptist!" For Jesus knew his frame and remembered that he was dust.

John had preached a victorious Messiah with fan in hand, purging his floor, gathering his wheat into the garner but burning the chaff with unquenchable fire. And here was Jesus, not carrying on that way at all but meek and lowly, going about doing good. And John couldn't figure it out. The devil got in his doubts as in Eden. John began wondering and then worrying, for one begets the other.

Our Lord's answer to John's question is simple. The blind are seeing, the deaf are hearing, the lame are walking, the lepers are being cleansed, and the poor have the gospel preached to them. In other words, "I am running on schedule and carrying out my program as planned. It may not be as you expected, but do not be upset by it."

This is a day of dungeons, and many saints are in the clutches of Giant Despair. There is comfort here for us. If a husky Lion Heart like John the Baptist could faint, "brethren, think it not strange concerning the fiery trial that is to try you, as though some strange thing happened unto you." Your temptation is common unto man and there is a way of escape.

John's trouble, like most trouble, did not come singly; it was twofold. There was depression and there was doubt. Dungeons bring depression and depression brings doubt. Are you in a dungeon? Not behind visible lock and key perhaps, but while "stone walls do not a prison make nor iron bars a cage," it is also true that other things than prison walls do a prison make and other than iron bars may form a cage. Is your trouble financial? Maybe your blood pressure is up and your bank account down. Maybe you are physically ill but you keep going and everyone thinks because you are walking you are well! Maybe you have lost a loved one and a shroud of melancholy hangs heavy on your soul. Perhaps you dread to see night fall and search for rest as men seek for hidden treasure. Dungeons bring depression, and from depression it is easy to move into doubt, even doubt about Jesus. Then we are upset and offended and we need to learn the forgotten beatitude.

It is nothing new to be offended in Jesus. More people have been offended in him than in any character in history. Away with this milk-and-water preaching about Jesus! He has caused more offense than any other person who ever lived. He is either a sanctuary or a stumbling stone (Isa. 8:14). He was an offense to his own nation and still is (Rom. 9:33). He offended the Pharisees (Matt. 15:12). He offended the people of his own home town (Matt. 13:54-58). He offended superficial disciples (John 6). His cross is an offense (1 Cor. 1:23). And even true disciples may be offended in him (Matt. 26:31-35). Sound believers sometimes get into a dungeon and pout with the Lord and say, "It is vain to serve God, and what profit is it that we have kept his ordinances and walked mournfully before the Lord of Hosts."

Don't you look pious, for we all have done it! We have murmured that we pray and do not receive. We gave our tithe and now we are in adversity. We were faithful to the Lord's house and landed in a hospital. We prayed for our children and they became worldlings. We craved joy and peace but we are despondent. Across the street is an ungodly family that has suffered no loss, while our dearest was taken. "There is no use in praying. It reads very lovely in the devotional books, but I seem unable to make it work." We were in distress, and the Lord "abode where he was," and when he did appear we grumbled like Martha when she said, "If thou hadst been here my brother had not died."

All such grumbling means that we have not learned the forgotten beatitude. Anybody can believe during fair weather. There is a deeper experience and a higher state which not many reach, a state in which, no matter what happens, we are never offended in the Lord—a state in which, whether it makes sense to us or not, we still believe Romans 8:28. Habakkuk started his book pouting and ended it praising. And blessed is the man who can say: "Though I don't get what I want; though I may sow much and reap little; though others get the plums and I get the sack, I will rejoice in the Lord, I will joy in the God of my salvation."

When Thomas asked for visible evidence of the risen Lord, he was asking for a smaller blessing than he already had, the privilege of believing without seeing, for "blessed are they that have not seen and yet have believed." God wants us to trust him, no matter what he does. There is a heavenly carelessness that leaves it all with Jesus and doesn't become upset when he does things contrary to what we expected. And there will be plenty of things that just don't make sense. John the Baptist must have wondered, "If Jesus can raise the dead, why can't he get me out of jail?" The little boy who couldn't understand why God put so many vitamins in spinach and didn't put them all in ice cream was already beginning to see that things just don't work out as we'd like for them to. There is much that is baffling; but if we can't understand it, by grace we can stand under it, we can see to it that we are not offended and that is better than understanding it! Some things we are to know (Matt. 13:11) and some things we are not to know (Acts 1:7), and we would be happier if we spent the time we waste on trying to fathom the unknowable in learning the knowable.

God did not explain suffering to Job. He gave him revelation, which was better than explanation. Better than having all our questions answered is to say, "The Lord knows what he is doing and I will not be offended."

In this dark hour of world distress not a few believers are in the dumps. Jesus seems not to be carrying on as expected. The world is not being converted. Has Christ failed? He isn't transforming the social order. Is he the One or shall we look for another? Many have been mistaught and have misunderstood his mission, his motive, his message, his method. It is true that he is not converting the world. He didn't say he would. But he has not failed; he is running on schedule. Blind eyes are opening to the Light of the world. Deaf ears are hearing his voice. Lame souls are taking up their beds and walking. Lepers, like Naaman of old, are dipping in Jordan and coming up with flesh like that of a little child. The dead in trespasses and sins are awaking to Christ, their Life and Light, and to the poor the gospel is still being preached. Christ is carrying on as intended. He has never missed an appointment. He may seem slow but he is never late. We need not be offended because he is not converting the world. He didn't promise to, but he did promise to return in clouds of glory and reign until all enemies are put under his feet. Let us therefore take our stand on his Word and hide it in our hearts, for "great peace have they which love thy law: and nothing shall offend them."

# CHAPTER 6

# You'll Get Over It!

*"I have somewhat against thee, because thou hast left thy first love"*
*(Revelation 2:4).*

Both in the world of nature and in the world of human nature we have a habit of getting over things. Whether for good or ill, the law of recovery is always at work.

Here is a landscape devastated by flood or hurricane. Crops are ruined, trees are uprooted, everything is wrecked by a mad upheaval, as though Mother Nature had run wild in a fit of temper. It looks as though the view could never be lovely again. But the months pass, and after awhile grass grows again and flowers bloom again and fresh crops are grown, and soon you would never know that there had been a disaster. For Nature tenderly heals her wounds, she gets over it.

Walking over battlefields of other days, one sees the healing of the scars of conflict. We have to look carefully to see the marks of former wars; and, although it will take longer this time, we trust that time will obliterate the wounds of this latest carnage. In England bomb explosions brought to light the seeds of plants that had not grown for years, and many varieties of flowers and shrubs sprang up in bomb craters as Nature wrought again her miracle of getting over it.

The human race has got over a lot of things. Wars and pestilences and famines have threatened to wipe us out and alarmists have cried, "We'll never be the same again!" but somehow we have survived. The human race has an astonishing power of recovery.

We individuals get over things. Some of us once were given up to die, riddled with disease, but we are still going—with some of our parts missing, maybe, but still "among those present." The hospitals have records of getting over it that fairly take one's breath. For Nature is the great restorer, and the moment you hurt your finger she rushes her repair force to the scene of trouble and will do wonders if given a chance.

We are always getting over things. Babies are very precious, but it is a good thing we get over our baby traits—if we do. It is natural for the baby to put things into its mouth indiscriminate-ly—and some of us never grow up in this regard, but we should. We can excuse the baby for putting a carpet tack in its mouth but what shall we say of grown-ups who put "coffin tacks" in theirs! It is natural for the baby to cry for what it wants; but if I should go down the street wailing for an ice-cream cone I should be inves-tigated, for "when I was a child, I spoke as a child, I understood as a child, I thought as a child," but having become a man I am supposed to have put away childish things. I have read of a man who boasted that at fifty years of age he still prayed the same prayer he used at five, "Now I lay me down to sleep...." Any man who has not found a better prayer than that in forty-five years ought to be ashamed of himself. He would be insulted if you told him that he had the mental development of a child of five; he would be a monstrosity if he had the body of a child of five, yet he prides himself on the spiritual development of a five-year-old!

Someone has said, "When a man grows up and doesn't grow up, he is a fool." A lot of trouble is caused by people who don't grow up. They look normal and would resent being called cases of arrested development, but they make others miserable by child-ish traits and tantrums which they should have outgrown long ago. If some middle-agers dressed according to their dispositions they would still be wearing rompers and pigtails!

But the law of recovery works both ways. While we get over things we should get over, we also get over things we should not get over. Many a man starts out in his chosen profession with noble ideals and high dreams; but the years take their toll, the perversity of humanity discourages him, the monotony of life depresses him, until what started as a golden consecration ends in a grouchy cynicism.

Sometimes old ministers grow bitter and sour. They started out brightly enough, but they saw so much of the evil of men's hearts that they were disappointed in men they once trusted; they had the Spirit quenched within them, until they became human wet blankets, saying to every young enthusiast, "Yes, I used to feel that way; you'll get over it!"

But not all preachers get over it. Some carry their springtime zeal through summer and autumn into the snows of winter, mellowed and refined, but still aflame. "The devil has no happy old men," but real Christians become more childlike—not childish—as the years go by.

Indeed, our Lord said, "Except ye be converted and become as little children, ye shall not enter into the kingdom of heaven," and I am sure that one thing he meant for us to see in that is that children have not become used to living—they are still fresh and full of expectancy. Life is crammed with surprises. They have not got used to it. Of course, we have a crop of youngsters today who get over it far too soon and become blasé and fed-up before they are out of their teens; but I am speaking of normal children. And a Christian ought to live with a sense of wonder, always expecting God to do some marvelous thing. We really do not expect much from God these days. We pray for rain and leave our umbrellas at home. We pray for revival but don't really expect one to start today. We have been told that whatsoever we ask in prayer, believing, we shall receive; but we ask, doubting, or, at the most, we ask, merely hoping, and our expectation is not unto him.

Right here was the trouble at Ephesus. She had got over her first love. Married couples do that today: bliss turns to boredom and ends in a divorce court. The same thing happens in the church. Ephesus had started out on fire for God. She was still orthodox and busy but something was lacking. She needed a revival. Many a church has started out with a few saints aflame for God, but later they became rich and increased with goods with need of nothing. They may still be doctrinally sound and religiously active but they have got over their first love and they need to remember and repent and repeat the first works.

Mind you, modernism and worldliness are not the only evils in the church today. There is a dreadful state among orthodox Christians whose doctrine is as sound as a dollar and who could not be called worldly by any stretch of the imagination, but who have become fed-up and heavy until they are harder to arouse than the grossest sinners. They have read so much and heard so much that nothing surprises them. They have lost their capacity for being stirred. Their reaction to any sermon is, "We have heard all the preachers and read all the books. Nothing that you could say would be new. We are veterans and we don't propose to get excited. We've heard all this and got over it and so will you." That sort of thing is hard on a young Timothy, and if he doesn't let God use him to get them out of their state the devil will use them to get him out of his!

The history of the church is a story of getting over it. Senator Borah said there were two stages in every movement, the apostolic and the mechanistic. The church has her periods of great awakening, when the fires of apostolic zeal burn high. Then the fires die, she becomes settled and complacent and mechanical. She gets over it. And the Lord has to send an awakener to rouse her again.

We individual Christians get over it. We leave our first love, we lose the joy of salvation, we get to where grace does not appear as precious as the hour we first believed. We get used to it, and while we recite the phrases and sing the songs, the color and freshness are gone. We take it all as a matter of course; we become like those iron fountains of A. J. Gordon's illustration, in which the water gushes out of iron lips that never taste it! If we were honest, we would sing:

Where is the blessedness I knew
When first I saw the Lord?
Where is the soul-refreshing view
Of Jesus and his Word?"

It is not necessary for us to fall into heresy or gross worldliness to get over it. We may believe the truth, stand for the truth, and yet in the very activities of the truth grow so accustomed to the truth that we "traffic in unfelt truth."

Christmas Evans, the great Welsh preacher, riding horseback one Saturday afternoon on his way to preach, was "convicted of a cold heart." He tethered his horse and spent hours in the woods in prayer until his heart thawed out "like the breaking up of a hard winter." He had "got over it," but, unlike some of us, he found it out. A preacher had better stop in his tracks if he finds himself moving from the apostolic to the mechanistic stage; he had better do something radical then and there. He had better drop everything and get into the woods with his Bible and read until he has a new Bible and pray until he has a new prayer, and come back a new man with a new message. A lot of churches think they need a new preacher when they simply need the same preacher renewed. Many a preacher thinks he needs a new pastorate when he needs to be renewed in the same pastorate. Robertson of Brighton wanted to resign from the ministry, but God impressed him that what he needed was to have his commission re-signed.

Not every preacher loses out because he went into false doctrine or had a moral breakdown. Some leave their first love in a round of church duties. Perhaps more leave it that way than in any other, for it is so deceptive: they are not aware of getting over it. They work at it harder than ever, but the harder they work, the farther they get from the thing they started out to do. The church at Ephesus was not having bingo instead of prayer-meetings. They were a fundamental, hard-working crowd, getting farther away all the time from the thing that mattered most, their love for Christ. We seem to think that the very momentum of

Christian activity will keep us in spiritual trim, but it carries us away from what we started out to do and be. We Christian workers sometimes assume that just because we are in the midst of spiritual labours all the time, that will keep us warm for Christ. But nothing is more dangerous; for familiarity with the things of God, if it does not breed contempt, may breed complacency. We get over it.

Whether church or preacher or layman, we had better watch lest our hands outrun our hearts, lest we let the abounding iniquity of this age make our love wax cold. Some think it a mark of maturity to be unresponsive to revival; it is a mark of that Laodicean lukewarmness that nauseates the Lord.

We had better get back to it, for all our activity is useless if we leave our first love. All our meetings, our rallies, our reunions are sounding brass and clanging cymbal until we recover that. We try to make up for it by adding more committees, drives, and picnics; but adding more wheels is a poor way to make up for having less steam!

It amounts to this: what we need is a revival. If you can't have one in your church get alone with God and have one yourself. Tell him you're slipping, getting over it, getting used to being a Christian, and that you don't like it. Get back past all the world confusion and church quarrels and differences among the saints and the weaknesses of the brethren, back to Christ, to one you can trust. Come to him afresh and fall in love with him again and get such an eye-full and heart-full of him that you feel like you did when you were converted. If it brings tears to the eyes and a tremor to the voice and an "amen" to the lips, well and good. If someone thinks you're having softening of the brain, tell them it is softening of the heart, and that you're getting over "hardening of the hearteries." Maybe you will strike fire in other hearts and start a revival. Certainly you will come nearer doing so than by criticizing the preacher, watching the faults of the deacons and the frailties of the missionary society.

Whatever it costs, no price is too great to kindle aflame the fires of our first love. If you are getting over it, heed the call of our

Christ: Remember and Repent and Repeat, "or else..." There is another R: He will "Remove" you from your place of usefulness. Many churches, many preachers, many Christians are on the shelf, disapproved, because they would not learn their three R's.

The only way to keep from getting over it is to get back to it!

# CHAPTER 7

# Our Threefold Commission

I revel in the story of our Lord's appearances during those for-ty wonderful days after his resurrection. How I would have enjoyed being there! Think of it! You might meet Jesus risen from the dead around any bend of the road!

Then I remember that he appeared only to believers. Why didn't he go to Herod or Pilate and say, "Look! You thought you had done away with me, but I'm back!" That wouldn't have been like Jesus. He made himself known only to his own, and if others are to hear about him today you and I must tell them.

Talk about a news story! Here is the greatest piece of news on earth! Jesus died and rose again! It is true, he really did it! They buried him dead and he came back alive! It is the greatest news flash in history, but we Christians have got used to it. We've heard it until we've lost the thrill of it. We've mixed it up with Easter corsages, bunny rabbits, spring bonnets, and colored eggs.

We hear much of the Great Commission, but we have three commissions. To the women at the sepulcher the angel said, "Go tell his disciples" (Mark 16:7). WE HAVE A MESSAGE FOR A BEWILDERED CHURCH. These disciples were bewildered. Jesus had died; their dreams had faded; their hopes had vanished. They didn't know what to think. They couldn't put it together. Some had gone back to their old pursuits, shaking their heads. They were trying to live on the memory of a dead Christ and when that is all you have, you are bewildered indeed.

But they were no more bewildered than the church today. Everywhere, Christians are confused, mystified, befuddled. Some are so taken up with their own problems that they cannot help others. Others are so busy trying to solve everybody else's problems that they have no time for their own. Some are chasing fads and isms, isms that soon become "wasms," out of date. Some churches are merely swapping members, moving corpses from one mausoleum to another. Some have made the gospel a funeral and others have made it a frolic, and both have forgotten that it is a feast! Some freeze and some fry!

But we have a message for a bewildered church: "Go tell his disciples that he goeth before you." The message is simply Christ. We need a new experience of the living Christ. He is not behind us in a tomb, he is ahead of us.

Consider the appearance of Jesus to Mary in the garden. First, there was a MISERY: "Woman, why weepest thou?" How many miserable Christians there are today! There was a MYS-TERY: Mary didn't know where to find her Lord. So many today are out of touch with Jesus, not living in vital communion. Then, when Mary recognized him, she called him MASTER. The cure for the MISERY is to see the Master and acknowledge him. But there was also a MISSION: "Go to thy brethren and say...." When we meet the Master, he commissions us.

The church needs to see Jesus. "Then were the disciples glad when they saw the Lord," not when they looked at each other. He is not real in our churches. If he were, we would not sit so lifelessly on Sunday, content with our formal uprisings and down-sittings, and go out as though we had met to honor a corpse instead of to hail a conqueror.

When we see him we shall quit looking at ourselves—and that ought to be a great relief. Some time ago, sitting in church, I gazed for a moment at a bright light overhead; and then when I looked around at the people I could see only the reflection of that light in their faces. And I wondered whether if we looked more at him we should not see more of him in our fellow Christians.

The bewildered church needs to see him going on before. He is our Joshua, our Leader. The church has never had so many would-be leaders as today. Some small boys were asked, "What are you playing?" "War," they answered. "But you are not doing much fighting." "No," they replied, "we are all generals." The church is overstaffed with generals. We need more and better privates. Everybody wants to pioneer, to start something. We have so many new movements that we can't move! We need to see our File-Leader going before us.

We have a second commission: "Go tell his disciples AND PETER." WE HAVE A MESSAGE FOR BACKSLIDING CHRISTIANS. Peter was a backslider, and the Lord singled him out as though he were marked "Special." He was not out to get even with Peter but to restore him. We put such characters in the doghouse. We fire them out, but Jesus fired them up with new love and zeal.

What a field day for the gossips that must have been when Peter denied Jesus! Can't you imagine them whispering to each other, "Have you heard the latest? Rev. Simon Peter swore that he never knew Jesus. I never had much confidence in him and now I'm through with him forever." But our Lord didn't feel that way about his wayward disciple. We need an Anti-vivisection Society in our churches, considering the way we dissect our brethren who sin not unto death instead of praying for them.

If you are a backslider the Lord is looking for you. When Jesus met Peter he asked him, "Lovest thou me?" He made himself the issue. The message for backsliders is just this: they need to see Jesus. We lambaste the erring or we ignore them. Jesus did neither. He did not begin by asking Peter, "Aren't you ashamed of yourself?" He asked, "Do you love me?" To begin with, on the night Peter denied Jesus, it was a look and not a lecture that sent Peter out to weep bitterly. We skin the saints alive on card-playing, dancing, theater-going, and we don't get very far. After all, you don't have to discuss such questions with people who really love the Lord. It is the wilderness crowd, seeking garlic instead of glory, melons instead of miracles, that asks, "What is wrong with this? Why is it wrong to do that?" People who are over in the Land, keeping step with our Joshua, never ask such questions. A man who is really living on figs and pomegranates, milk and honey, is not likely to start sighing for the fleshpots of Egypt. The real issue in separation is not quitting this or that, but "let us go forth unto him." The issue is Christ. "Lovest thou ME?" Backslider, you have an appointment with Jesus and the sooner you get together, the better.

We have a third commission, the Great Commission to go into all the world and make disciples. WE HAVE A MESSAGE FOR A BENIGHTED WORLD. And that message is Christ. He is the Center: "All power is given unto me; Lo, I am with you." The world is the circumference. In his interview with Peter he was the center: "Lovest thou ME?" But there was also the circumference: "Feed my sheep." In geometry we use a compass. One prong is stationary, fixed. With the other we describe our circle. Christ is the fixed center, the same yesterday, today, forever. From that center we make the sweep of the whole world as our circumference. "What the world needs is Jesus," "We've a story to tell to the nations," and we are out to win them not to a way of life or even to Christianity, but to Christ.

We have SOMETHING BACK OF US: "All power is given unto me in heaven and in earth." There are our resources. Our Lord always makes his propositions against the background of his resources. "All things are delivered unto me of my Father.... Come unto me" (Matt. 11:27, 28). Again, "The Father loveth the Son and hath given all things into his hand. He that believeth on the Son hath everlasting life" (John 3:35, 36). And here is the Great Commission: "All power is given unto me.... Go." Put them together and we have, "All things are mine: come, believe, go." And that is the full Christian experience.

There is not only something back of us, there is SOME-THING BEFORE US: "all the world." And we also have SOMEONE WITH US: "Lo, I am with you." And let us not forget that our message is Christ himself. We try to match the world's wit and cleverness. We try to meet it on its own ground and amuse it and entertain it. We give it a glorified hash, a religious mulligan stew of ethics and psychology and philosophy. We forget that what we have that the world doesn't have is Jesus. There is no point in trying to meet it with something it already has. We are ministers, not mimics; apostles, not apes. We are to let our light shine, and that light is Christ. It is a glow, not a glare; and we do not shine it, we let it shine.

"Go tell the disciples; go tell Peter; go tell the world." And tell them about Jesus, dead, risen, and alive forevermore!

CHAPTER 8

# Down From Above

*"And he said unto them, Ye are from beneath; I am from above: ye are of this world; I am not of this world" (John 8:23).*

From beginning to end, the Bible teaches that God works down from above, not up from below. This, of course, is contrary to human reasoning. Man teaches that we are on our way from the bottom to the top, that we started as sentient jelly on the shoreland of some prehistoric age and that through millions of years of evolution we have been working our way up from below. But God says that in his dealings with us from start to finish he works down from above.

To begin with, God says that man was made in God's image, but he fell. And when he fell, he did not fall upward. Adam started better than he finished. He was not a caveman swinging a club but a Godlike being who fell. "In Adam all die." "By one man sin entered into the world and death by sin." "All have sinned and come short of the glory of God."

For quite a while we have been taught that man started with no knowledge of God but that he has worked his way up through animism, fetishism, totemism, polytheism; that in the Jewish nation he reached monotheism and in Jesus Christ he carried that idea to its highest ideals. But the truth is, man started with a knowledge of God; but when he knew God he glorified him not as God neither was thankful, but became vain in his imagination, so that his foolish heart was darkened and professing himself to be wise he became a fool. The first chapter of Romans presents us with a picture of degradation and depravity that forever debunks the idea that man has been continually seeking God's fellowship

49

through the ages. Even the Israelites, when they did know God, were continually turning from God to idols. Such has been the course of church history. Such has been individual experience. The human heart is deceitful and desperately wicked, and its natural bent is away from God. "The carnal mind is enmity against God: for it is not subject to the law of God, neither indeed can be." "The natural man receiveth not the things of the Spirit of God: for they are foolishness unto him: neither can he know them, because they are spiritually discerned." Men hate God. They do not want God, they resent him, they are rebels against him, they make gods of their own.

Whoever assumes that man is kindly disposed toward God, and that if God's love be presented and the winsomeness of Christ be preached, men will fall over each other rushing down church aisles to be saved, is in for a big surprise. The facts simply do not bear that out. God's Word does not teach it. It is not true to history or experience. Jesus Christ lived among us in all his winsomeness and we spat upon him, crowned him with thorns, crucified him on a tree. And we would do it again. He said the world hated him and that it would hate us. And the reason it does not hate us Christians more is not because the world today is more like Christ but because we Christians are so unlike him.

Man is not on his way up but on his way down. It is ridiculous to ask man to follow Christ so long as he is unsaved. He is a guilty sinner and must be made to face the fact; he must see himself as God sees him. Then will he pray like David, "Against thee, thee only, have I sinned." We must stop dusting off sin with a powder puff and spreading cold cream over the cancers of iniquity. Sin is not mere imperfection, the leftovers of a brute ancestry. Man is not evolving Godward. Left to himself, he is foul, reprobate, degenerate, disgusting, not on his way up to heaven but on his way down to hell.

Certainly the Word of God paints no rosy picture of man in his natural state. Instead, we are told, "The whole head is sick, and the whole heart faint. From the sole of the foot even unto the head there is no soundness in it; but wounds and bruises and putrifying sores: they have not been closed, neither bound up, neither mollified with ointment." If it be objected that this is an Old Testament picture of a corrupt nation we turn to the New Testament and find the human race given over by God to "a reprobate mind, to do those things which are not convenient; being filled with all unrighteousness, fornication, wickedness, covetousness, maliciousness; full of envy, murder, debate, deceit, malignity; whisperers, backbiters, haters of God, despiteful, proud, boasters, inventors of evil things, disobedient to parents, without understanding, covenant-breakers, without natural affection, implacable, unmerciful; who knowing the judgment of God, that they which commit such things are worthy of death, not only do the same, but have pleasure in them that do them." Again, if it be objected that we have made progress since Paul wrote Romans, we turn to his description of men in the last days and find that men are no better, that these same characteristics persist and some more are thrown in for good measure. Lovers of their own selves, covetous, boasters, proud, blasphemers, disobedient to parents, unthankful, unholy, without natural affection, truce-breakers, false accusers, incontinent, fierce, despisers of those that are good, traitors, heady, high-minded, lovers of pleasures more than lovers of God—these, mind you, are marks of the human race at the end of its course. Man still is no better. For it is not a progressive race "evoluting" upward but a perishing race "deviluting" downward. Of course, that is not what we are reading in popular magazines; it is not what starry-eyed idealists are telling us—but it is what God says.

Man's teaching makes him think well of himself. God's Word makes him think meanly of himself but well of Jesus Christ. A lady who objected to proofs of her picture on the grounds that they didn't do her justice was told by the photographer, "Lady, what you need is not justice but mercy." That is what man needs, and God shows him his just deserts that he may offer him mercy.

So there are two schools of thought with us: that man in his present state is on his way up from the beast, or that he is on his way down from the best. If the first is correct he needs only culture; if the second be true he needs Calvary. If the first is correct, he needs only education; if the second, he needs regeneration. If we believe God, man needs Calvary—and that brings us to the next consideration.

In his dealings with us God works down from above, not up from below. Consider that OUR SAVIOUR CAME DOWN FROM ABOVE. "The first man is of the earth, earthy: the second man is the Lord from heaven" (1 Cor. 15:47). "I came down from heaven, not to do mine own will, but the will of him that sent me" (John 6:38). "I am from above" (John 8:23).

Right here is a problem that stumps the evolutionist. If we are evolving upward all the while, why did the perfect Man appear almost two thousand years ago? Why can't we produce a greater character than Jesus Christ? We've had almost twenty centuries since he appeared and we haven't had a man who can say, "Which of you convinceth me of sin?"

Jesus Christ was not a step in the upward evolution of man from below. He was an intervention of God from above! Man was ruined and on his way down and couldn't save himself, but God so loved the world that he broke into the course of things and introduced another order of life, a supernatural Christ, his only begotten Son, to rescue man from going down and to lift him up. Jesus Christ was not merely the best man who ever lived, on his way up from below. He was the Son of God come down from heaven to die for our sins and rise again.

In this day when people are asking, "What must I do to succeed?" instead of "What must I do to be saved?" they ask, "Why do we need a Savior? Aren't we on our way up by science and invention?" Well, we are going places with our heads and hands but we have outrun our hearts. Indeed, we have come from tallow candles to television, but what does man do with his inventions? He goes wild and cuts his own throat with them! Have we not just seen two highly intelligent nations go crazy and wreck the world?

Man's heart is not right. He is on his way down, spiritually, and unless his course is changed he will end down and not up.

Only God can change that course. That is why he sent his Son from above that whosoever believeth in him should not perish, for perish is exactly what he will do otherwise. Jesus Christ could never save us if he were only a man, even if he were the best man. He had to be another kind of man, the God-man. So God broke in from above. He had to start a new race with a new Adam, for the first race had failed. That new Adam is the Lord from heaven, and to as many as receive him power is given to become the sons of God, members of a new race on its way up instead of down.

How is this change accomplished? Here again God works from above. "Except a man be born from above he cannot see the kingdom of God" (John 3:3). THE NEW BIRTH IS FROM ABOVE. What man needs is not a boost from below but a birth from above! He doesn't like to be told that he needs a new birth. He tries to cover his sins and excuse his iniquities; but, for all his culture and progress, he is still only a savage with a thin veneer of civilization. He is on his way down and must be born from above. Even religious people find that hard to accept. Our Lord said to Nicodemus, "Art thou a master in Israel and knowest not these things?" There have been church members, deacons, elders, even preachers and missionaries, who were very slow to learn it. We argue from the natural that as the twig is bent so is the tree inclined. We bring in a lot of psychiatric jargon to explain our conduct, but all that is true in our newest findings along that line has been in the Bible all the while. There is a "wisdom that is FROM ABOVE" that brings in a higher law. By the law of gravitation my knife, when I drop it, falls to the floor. But by another law I throw it upward and it sticks to the ceiling. "Ah, but you interfered and did something to it," do I hear you say? Well, we were all headed downward by one law, but when we believe in Christ, God starts us upward by another law! God steps in and does something for us and to us and in us.

That is grace, and the natural man does not like to hear it. He wants to save himself; he does not like to be God's charity patient, coming just as he is without one plea but the shed blood of Christ. He does not like to be told that eternal life is a gift which he can neither earn nor learn. He thinks he is on his way up and needs a boost, but God says he is on the way down and needs a birth!

Finally, THE HEAVENLY CITY COMES DOWN FROM ABOVE. Man has been trying to build heaven on earth for a long time. From the Tower of Babel onward, he has created his paradises and Utopias, all kinds of experiments and projects, but his Babels have all come down in ruins. He is still at it. Years ago, Henry Drummond advanced the idea that the New Jerusalem could be any city, my city, your city, if we but make it so. And so by education, sanitation, ventilation, we strive to create here the perfect city. But God's Word says the New Jerusalem will not be built up from below. In fact, man's final civic masterpiece is described in Revelation. It is Babylon the Great, and it comes to a horrible finish. The terrible eighteenth chapter of the Apocalypse pictures the final chapter in the civic genius of unregenerate humanity. Babylon falls and becomes the habitation of devils, a plagued city full of death and mourning and fire, where the voice of music and industry shall be stilled and where light and joy shall disappear. In this day of atomic bombs, and with the ruins of Berlin and Tokyo fresh among us, it should not be difficult to visualize these fearful scenes. Some who ridiculed the lurid pictures from John on Patmos ought not find them to be so far-fetched now!

But soon after this awful portrayal of Babylon's doom John writes: "And I John saw the holy city, new Jerusalem, COMING DOWN FROM GOD OUT OF HEAVEN, prepared as a bride adorned for her husband." Once again God breaks in from above. We do not build up the ideal city from below. Of course, we don't like to be told that. Of course, all social reformers and planners and dreamers and experts who have never seen God's blueprints will dismiss them as a lot of apocalyptic wildfire as out of date as the notion that the earth is flat and four-cornered. Now, to be sure, this does not mean that Christians are not to work to make our present cities as decent as possible. We do not expect perfect law and order in this age, but we should co-operate with whatever agencies we do have for maintaining the peace. Nevertheless, we know that unregenerate man cannot build the New Jerusalem. If he could, what would he do with it? They told us a few years ago that the machine age would set us all at leisure to cultivate the finer things. But what does the average man do with leisure when he gets it? He gets drunk or plays bridge or goes to a silly show or sits up half the night reading trash. What would such people do in the New Jerusalem? If the human race in its present state moved into the New Jerusalem today it would be hell by tomorrow!

Heaven is a prepared place for a prepared people, built by God for the people of God, and it comes down from above for a people born from above by faith in him who came down from above.

Peter tells us about "the world that was," a world destroyed by water. He tells us that the heavens and earth which exist now are literally stored with fire which will destroy them. Then he tells us, "Nevertheless we, according to his promise, look for new heavens and a new earth, wherein dwelleth righteousness." True to his prophecy, scoffers are now among us reminding us that things continue as they were from the beginning of the creation. But we have had one world destroyed by water, we are in a world to be destroyed by fire, and we look for a new world, a heavenly city come down from above. Anything else is willful ignorance, as Peter plainly declares.

Thanks be unto God, who works from above. See to it that you have been born from above. Then, "if ye be risen with Christ, seek those things which are above, where Christ sitteth on the right hand of God. Set your affections on things above, not on things on the earth. For ye are dead and your life is hid with Christ in God."

# CHAPTER 9

# "What Doest Thou Here?"

Elijah had come out of a big day on Carmel. He had prayed down fire and water and had become the outstanding man of his generation. It was a red-letter day for the prophet. But the next day after a big day may be a very bad day. From his baptism our Lord moved into his temptation. In the same chapter that tells us of Paul's third heaven experience we read of his thorn in the flesh. So we move rapidly from height to depth and must needs watch the next day after our Carmels.

Jezebel had threatened Elijah, his nerves had gone into a tailspin, and under the juniper he imagined himself to be the surviving saint, the last good man. There are three great chapters in the life of this prophet and they might well be titled, Cherith, Carmel, and the Cave. In the cave the Lord asks him, "What doest thou here?"

Not a few of the saints are in a cave today and we would inquire of them, "What doest thou here?" For one thing, ELIJAH WAS TIRED, and so are many of God's people. God did not reprove Elijah. He fed him, rested him, and said, "The journey is too great for thee." It is too much for most of us these days. Never have I preached to so many tired people as now. The human race lives in a nervous breakdown. It is a day of stress, strain, and tension; and our very speech is the speech of weariness, the language of languor. We are weary and faint in our minds. Fatigue is filling hospitals, asylums, graves. Men cannot drink it away with whiskey nor play it away at card tables nor laugh it off in a theatre nor sleep it away with sedatives. Our remedies treat only the symptoms and not the disease.

An old lady who was asked why she didn't sue for damages after being hurt in an auto wreck replied, "I got enough damages, what I need is repairs." She was stating our case today. What we need is repairs. The journey is too great even for us Christians. Sometimes I have thought I would like to start a Bible conference for Bible conference speakers. The theme verse would be, "Why gaddest thou about so much?" (Jer. 2:36).

The prophet speaks to edification, exhortation, and comfort. He strengthens, stirs, soothes, and the saints need all three. We are to grow in grace, and growth involves food, rest, and exercise. Some feed all the time and need to exercise and work off some of the sermons with which they have stuffed themselves. But others exercise too much and need rest. The Christian life is not a glorified St. Vitus's dance. We are to be willing disciples, not whirling dervishes. Elijah ate and slept. When we cannot do that we are not worth much to God or man.

The Bible has as much to say about resting as about working. We need to come apart and rest awhile, and if we don't come apart, we will come apart, we'll go to pieces! It is true that the devil never takes a vacation, but we are not to follow the devil but the Lord. Jesus was never in a hurry, and we need to learn the gait of Galilee. John Wesley said, "I do not have time to be in a hurry." Some of the saints tear around until you would think the world would go to pieces if they stopped. But soon they end in a hospital, they blow out a fuse. They go up like rockets and down like rocks. They would do more if they did less. Quantity production is an American standard, not a Bible standard.

Our Lord asked, "Are there not twelve hours in the day?" There is always time enough to do what God wants done. What takes so much time is doing what we want to do. "He that believeth shall not make haste." The slow hand on the watch is the most important hand. Too many, like Ahimaaz, want to run before they have any tidings ready; and when they arrive they can report only a tumult. About all the average go-getter ever gets is high blood pressure and a heart attack. Idleness is the devil's workshop, but so is busyness if one tries too much.

Elijah was tired and so are we, and we shall honor God by resting. We are not to say there are four months until harvest, for now is God's time; but there are twelve hours in the day, there is time enough in God's time to do his will. And part of his will is to rest. "He who waits on God loses no time."

Elijah was also DISCOURAGED and PESSIMISTIC. He thought he was the last good man, and needed to learn that God had seven thousand who had not bowed to Baal. When we are too tired we easily grow despondent and imagine that everybody is out of step except ourselves. It is true that few there be who find the way of life, but they are not so few as we sometimes think. We sometimes undertake to sift out the saints ourselves and consign to perdition all who do not cross their "t's" and dot their "i's" as we do. These seven thousand were probably silent believers, who shouldn't have been so hidden that nobody knew they were in existence. They should have stood with Elijah in such an evil day. But, still, they were known to God, if not to Elijah, and we need to remember that the Lord knoweth them that are his. He will deal with them for being cowards and not letting their light shine, but we do not need to get down in the dumps and put a bushel over our own testimony on their account.

There are more good people than we sometimes think. It was two rather indefinite disciples, Joseph of Arimathea and Nicodemus, who buried Jesus after some more positive believers had forsaken him and fled. After all, it is not for us to number the Lord's people.

Furthermore, ELIJAH WAS SUFFERING A REACTION FROM A BIG AND NOISY DAY ON CARMEL. Here we run into a very important issue these days. The prophet's nerves had let down, and the threat of Jezebel finished the blow. From Carmel to a cave was quite a change, but he needed to hear the still, small voice. We Americans need to hear it. We are sold on noise and size, even in our churches, and this voice turns the tables on both standards, for it is STILL and SMALL We are sold on NOISE but this is a STILL voice. "He shall not cry nor lift up nor cause his voice to be heard in the street." His

Spirit is compared with a dove. The greatest things make the least noise. The sun draws millions of gallons of water with less noise than we make getting a bucketful out of a well. Did you ever hear the planets go round or the sun rise or the dew fall? We do not hear God's whisper because we are listening for wind, fire, and earthquake. We should "study to be quiet." We cannot endure solitude because we are in such poor company when we are alone! We cannot contemplate. Watch the average tourist galloping through an art gallery! It is the quiet pool and not the rushing stream that reflects the stars. "He leadeth me beside the STILL waters."

Said Newton D. Baker:

"The effect of modern inventions has been to immeasurably increase the difficulty of deliberation and contemplation on large and important issues. I doubt whether there could have been a Constitution of the United States of America if the deliberations of the Constitutional Conventions had been currently reported by radio, telegraph, and newspapers over the whole extent of the thirteen colonies."

This noise standard shows up in our churches. Some of us think we are not having a good meeting unless there is a lot of hullabaloo. Oh, I know that what some call worship is just the device by which some resters at ease in Zion catch up with their sleep. And what some call reverence and dignity is just spiritual rigor mortis, the Sunday coma of religious dopesters getting their eleven o'clock dose of pulpit cocaine. But the counterfeit implies the true, and most of us are so feverish and nervous that we cannot hear God's whisper. "Be still and know that I am God." The Lord commanded the multitude to sit down before he fed them.

Then we are sold on size, and this voice of God is SMALL. Some think we must have a thousand people to have a revival. We worship the great god Ballyhoo and borrow our methods from the business and amusement and social worlds, trying to put over God's work by might and power instead of by his Spirit.

We need to study afresh David's unhappy experience in bringing the ark back to Jerusalem. He proposed the move to his captains and leaders, and "the thing was right in the eyes of the people," but we do not read that God was consulted. They put on a show, they had a crowd and a brass band and quite a demonstration, but it was a Philistine expedient and not God's way, and he brought it to nought. Today we make shows of some of our church conventions. We hire the biggest hall and get the governor to speak and try to impress the world by borrowing its tactics, but we only cheapen our cause and make ourselves ridiculous. God is not fooled by barnstorming claptrap. David would have got the ark to Jerusalem sooner if he hadn't been in such a hurry that he couldn't use God's method. We delay God's purposes by our expedients.

The Spirit blows where he will, and God is not bound to our grand ideas. The great Welsh revival was accomplished without preaching, without choirs, without hymn books, without organs, without publicity, and without offerings. These things are not evil, but God can do wonders without what we think he must have.

God does indeed speak in wind and fire and earthquake, through great movements and famed leaders. But they are more or less occasional, and he probably does his greatest work in quiet places and through humble lives. Many an Elijah who has learned the lesson of Cherith and Carmel still needs to learn the lesson of the cave. God does appear in the extraordinary. He does feed by ravens and send down fire from heaven. But sometimes he must shut up his servants in a cave to make them hear the still small voice.

We think of revival today in terms of great crowds and famous preachers. We would like to see the fire fall in a thundering demonstration of the power of God to vindicate his cause and put the hosts of sin to flight. But let us not be blind to the quiet movement of the Spirit in thousands whose work of faith and labor of love God will not forget. Blessed is the man who does not measure by noise and size. "In returning and rest shall ye be saved; in quietness and confidence shall be your strength."

Not only was Elijah tired and pessimistic and over-affected by noise and size. He was derelict in his duty. He had no business under the juniper. He needed to get back on the job. In God's permissive will he took mercy on the prophet and taught him a lesson, but Elijah should not have run from the threat of Jezebel. A man is first a runaway before he is a castaway.

"What doest thou here?" Are you under a juniper? Is the journey too great for you, and are you exhausted, tired on the way, though not tired of the way? Have you grown pessimistic until you imagine yourself the surviving saint? Have you been living on excitement, big days, and big demonstrations, fire and wind and earthquake, until you cannot hear God whisper? Has the threat of Jezebel driven you to the wilderness? Wait on the Lord and renew your strength! As important as it is to be saved and sure and sound and strong, don't forget how much it means to be still!

# CHAPTER 10

# Missing Notes in the Modern Church

It is very fashionable nowadays to ask, "What is wrong with the church?" It is no new subject. There has always been something or other wrong with the professing church, and there have always been speakers aplenty to discuss it. Unfortunately, their speaking usually relieves only the speaker and not the situation. One is reminded of the soapbox orator in London some years ago. He was lambasting the government with a vengeance. Somebody asked a policeman: "Why don't you do something with him?" "Oh, leave 'im alone," the bobby replied, "it relieves 'im and it don't 'urt us."

I venture to suggest three characteristics of the New Testament church that are out of style today. There are other marks of the early church that are also out of style, but one cannot cover everything in one message. I think that if we seriously considered these lost characteristics and recovered them we would be a long way toward answering the question, "What is wrong with the church?"

The New Testament church was an intolerant church. At once we throw ourselves open to a broadside of protest. "Intolerant" is a scandalous word to use these days, for if there is anything that is in style among our "progressive" churches it is that word "tolerance." You would think that intolerance was the unpardonable sin. We are majoring as never in all church history on being broad-minded. That we have become so broad we have become also pitifully shallow never seems to disturb us. We must "broaden or bust." Of course, some experts in tolerance can be amazingly intolerant of those who do not share their broad-mindedness, but that does not disturb them either.

There is, of course, a false, pharasaic intolerance that has no place in a true church. And one encounters it again and again among conservative Christians. It has brought about the remark that the modernists are arid and the fundamentalists are acrid, that the former lack clarity and the latter charity. It has nick-named the fundamentalists "feudamentalists" and gotten them a reputation for spending so much time sniping at each other that they have little time left to go after the devil.

But there is a proper intolerance, and the New Testament church had it. They were intolerant of any way of salvation except Jesus Christ. "Neither is there salvation in any other: for there is none other name under heaven given among men whereby we must be saved" (Acts 4:12). That makes it straight and narrow, and it isn't what you are hearing in some localities these days. You are hearing that Jesus is the best way but that other ways are good and will lead to God just the same. Union meetings of Catholics, Protestants, and Jews create the impression that a general faith in God is enough without specific faith in Christ. Now, that cannot be true if no man comes to the Father but by Christ. The devils believe that there is one God and tremble: men believe it and do not even tremble, but expect to reach heaven by theism instead of by Calvary.

The New Testament church was also intolerant of anything that threatened to compromise this gospel of no other name. In Galatia men tried to mix in a little legalism, and in Colosse they were slipping in a bit of false mysticism—and Paul would have none of it. He could have been very "lovely" about it and stylishly tolerant, and he could have said nothing about it. I am sure that some of the false teachers must have accused him of seeing bugaboos and hobgoblins. He could have told Timothy to play ball with the apostates of his day, but instead he wrote, "From such turn away." He advised Titus to reject a heretic after the first and second admonition, which sounds uncomfortably intolerant. And even the gentle John forbade hospitality to those who abode not in the doctrine of Christ, asserting that "he that biddeth him God speed is partaker of his evil deeds." To be sure, we are not advised to bawl him out and throw stones after him until he is out of sight: but neither is there any encouragement for that fashionable modern fellowship with unbelievers.

The New Testament church was intolerant of sin in its midst. When serious trouble first showed up in Ananias and Sapphira it was dealt with in sudden and certain terms. When immorality cropped out in Corinth Paul delivered the offender to the devil for the destruction of his flesh. It was in line with our Lord's teaching on discipline in the eighteenth chapter of Matthew. To be sure, it was to be done in love and tenderness; and the brother overtaken in a fault was to be restored by the spiritual ones, and Paul was quick to recommend the restoration of the Corinthian brother. But, still, sin was not to be glossed over and excused as we condone it today in our churches until liars, gamblers, drunkards, and divorcees fill prominent places in Sunday schools and on boards and have never as much as heard that we must be clean who bear the vessels of the Lord. We have let the camel get his foot in the door and then his head, until now the whole camel is inside and along with him other animals far more unsavory. Peter added even hogs and dogs to our spiritual zoology, and the lambs today are so mixed with every other species that what was once a sheepfold has become a zoo. Our Lord warned us that the shepherd who did not stand his ground when the wolves appeared was only a hireling. We are bidden to feed his sheep but not to feed wolves. I grant you that it is often a complicated problem and can be handled only on one's knees. But we are paying an awful price today for our sweet tolerance of sin within the church. If the church of the Acts had overlooked iniquity and bypassed evil and smilingly looked the other way while the devil sneaked into every phase of her life as we have done today, Christianity would have died in infancy.

The New Testament church had a healthy, holy intolerance. It got somewhere because it started out on a narrow road and stuck to it. It might easily have taken up a dozen wide boulevards and ended in destruction. We face the peril of the wide gate and the broad way today, and it tantalizes us all the more because "many there be which go in thereat." We were told a long time ago that "few there be" who take the S. and N. the Straight and Narrow. We Americans especially are gregarious; we like to run with the crowd. We had rather be called almost anything on earth than narrow; yet our Lord chose the adjective, and faithfulness to him will prove that it still fits today.

I am sure that there were those who called the early church "exclusive," and predicted that it would never get anywhere until it became inclusive. "Exclusive" is another word that is anathema today and has been shoved into the limbo of the outmoded, along with "intolerant" and "narrow." But the New Testament church was the most exclusive fellowship on earth. It was not just a society of people with good intentions. It was not a club for improving the old Adam. It was a fellowship of people who believed in Jesus Christ as the one and only Savior. It seemed not to have a chance in the face of the great Roman world. It could easily have let down the bars and taken in all sorts of religiously minded folk, but it stuck to "Jesus Only." A river may look very lovely spread out all over a marsh, but to generate power it must narrow itself. We have endeavored to spread out the river today. We have sacrificed depth for width and instead of a power dam we have a stagnant swamp.

In the second place, the New Testament church was not only intolerant, narrow, exclusive. IT WAS A REPELLENT CHURCH. Instead of attracting everybody, it repelled. In the fourth chapter of Acts the church was really going places for God. It was a great hour but dangerous. Could the church stand success? There is a turn in the story with the fifth chapter. It begins "But..." Ananias and Sapphira appear; trouble has arisen in the midst. There were plenty of liars in Jerusalem but these were in the church! But by the grace of God the church rose to the occasion and cleaned house. Ananias and Sapphira were carried out dead and the church rolled on. We read, "And great fear came upon all the church, and upon as many as heard these things. And by the hands of the apostles were many signs and wonders wrought among the people; and they were all with one accord on Solomon's porch." Here is the church in the full bloom of her power: a Spirit-filled church, a wonder-working (not a wondering!) church; a church that stirred up the devil.

Then we read that there were three reactions: first, "And of the rest durst no man join himself to them." People didn't join this church carelessly. They were afraid to. There was a holy awe that kept Tom, Dick, and Harry at a distance. People didn't rush into this fellowship just because it was the nice thing to do. It meant something to unite with this crowd. There was a holy repulsion, and I know of nothing that the church needs more today. It is the last thing we think we need. We are always trying to attract. Our programs, prizes, picnics, and pulpit pyrotechnics are aimed at drawing the people in. Here was a church that made people stand back! We have catered to the world, we have let the world slap the church on the back in coarse familiarity. Here was a church that prospered by repelling!

You will observe that all this followed on the heels of the death of Ananias and Sapphira. If the church took a stand today on sins within; if we thundered out, as Peter did here, against lying to the Holy Ghost, it would make the world stand at a respectful distance, and the fear of God would fall on a generation that laughs at the church. What was the sin of Ananias and Sapphira? They pretended to make a full consecration which was not real. And are not our churches filled with men and women who sing, "I surrender all," when they have not surrendered anything? The church is cluttered with people who should never have joined. She already has too many of the kind she has. We need a holy repulsion. You don't have to be different to be a church-member now. There is little about the average church to make men stand back in reverence. In other days we at least had church discipline. I can recall the old Saturday church meetings, when Ananias and Sapphira were dealt with. Some mistakes were made but there was a healthy regard for the sanctity of the church. When the church takes a stand, it repels careless "joiners."

But someone asks, "What would people think if we took such a stand?" Let us see what happened here: "But the people magnified them." The church had favor with all the people (Acts 2:47). The church that stands in the power of the Spirit wins the respect of the people. We have driven them away in trying to attract them. We have lost favor in trying to win favor. The world is sick and disgusted with the church making a clown of itself, trying to talk the slang of this age, running third-rate amusement parlors, playing bingo, and putting on rummage sales. The church, it has been said, is not running a show-boat but a life-boat, and we make ourselves ridiculous in trying to compete with the world. The preacher and church that stand for God and righteousness will be magnified.

When judgment fell on Ananias and Sapphira the world sat up and took notice. Today we coddle and excuse our sins, call weakness what God calls wickedness. We shelter sin in the church, and when a preacher would cry out against it he is advised, "Don't be too hard, nobody is perfect," and is given a dressing-down from the text, "Judge not that ye be not judged." We have let down the bars until anybody can get into a church and nobody ever gets out. If we raised the New Testament standard it would stop the rush of superficial disciples and win respect where now there is ridicule.

"But nobody would ever join!" do we hear? Let us see what happened here: "And believers were the more added to the Lord, multitudes both of men and women." While outsiders dared not join, the Lord added more and more to himself. The church that repels as this church repelled will attract as this church attracted. It will be the attraction of the Holy Spirit, and he will draw out those who really believe. All that is necessary is just to be New Testament Christians and a New Testament church, and we will both repel and attract. It is a law of nature. The rose has its thorns, it both repels and attracts. Everywhere you look in the world of nature, you observe this double law at work. It is a law of the spiritual world too.

What is this repulsion? There is a false repulsion. Often we drive people away by our indifference, criticism, lack of love and zeal. We ought to be ashamed of it, confess that we are ugly and unattractive Christians, repent of our bigotry, coldness, and hardness, and let the Lord make us winsome with the loveliness of Christ.

But there is a repulsion that goes with being a Christian. Here is a fine Christian girl, beautiful and charming in face, in mind, in spirit. When she comes into a gathering she is attractive. But there is also something about her which makes it out of the question to use profanity in her presence, something which makes the rudely familiar keep at a distance. She doesn't have to say, "I will allow no foul language, no improper advances." People just don't curse and otherwise misbehave in the presence of such people. She repels while she attracts.

There ought to be that about every Christian when he walks into a gathering, that makes the unholy and profane subdued and respectful. There ought to be that about a church that would make the world never dream of rudely rushing into its fellowship. And Jesus himself both attracts and repels. He is the great divider. He has attracted more people and driven more people away than any other character in all time. Once, when he had preached a crowd away, he asked the disciples: "Will ye also go away?" All through his ministry men were being drawn and repelled. The young ruler was first drawn; then when the terms of discipleship were made known, he was repelled.

God help us, as Christians and churches, to recover the power of God among us until a holy awe shall rest upon us. God help us to deal with sin until men shall be afraid to lie to the Holy Ghost. When we do, outsiders will not dare to join us; the people will magnify us; believers will be added to the Lord.

There is a third characteristic of the New Testament that is quite out of style: IT WAS A SENSATIONAL CHURCH. There was something happening every minute. On the day of Pentecost the multitude gathered "amazed, confounded, and perplexed." And from that day on, Jerusalem was kept in a turmoil on account of this new power let loose in the world which jails could not lock up nor swords kill nor death destroy. And wherever they went, these Christians stirred up the elements.

Paul exceedingly troubled Philippi and created no small stir in Ephesus and won the name of a world upsetter. That a mere handful of plain witnesses, talking about One who was supposed to be dead and buried, should tackle the great Roman world in a head-on collision and come off winners is the most sensational thing in history.

Today we Christians are living, for the most part, on the momentum with which the New Testament church started and on fresh waves of momentum started since through others who were sensational in their day. Savonarola and Luther and Knox and Wesley and Whitefield and Moody let nobody go to sleep in their vicinity. But of late anything out of the ordinary, anything likely to disturb the saints at ease in Zion, is frowned upon by a stiff and starched formalism "faultily faultless, icily regular, splendidly null." In reaction to that there has sprung up in the churches today an extreme sensationalism as bad as the thing it tries to correct. Wild free-lances, weird prophetic firebrands, erratic evangelists would try to remedy freezing in formalism by frying in emotionalism. So the battle rages, and the saints are so busy calling each other names that Satan gets scant attention.

But the counterfeit proves the genuine and the fact of a spurious sensationalism should not blind us to the truth. Someone has said that sensational preaching is the kind some preachers don't like because they can't do it. Be that as it may, we have dried up being "resolutionary," we need to become revolutionary. There is no reason why any band of Spirit-filled Christians should not arouse and excite and stir any community. If they didn't, something would be wrong. It is argued that the world is so much more Christian than it was in the New Testament days that we cannot expect such reactions today. The argument is beside the point. The days are darker instead of brighter and the contrast should be all the more pronounced. As for being Christian, our civilization has become infected with a mild rash of Christianity that has almost immunized it against the real thing. A real revival would be such a contrast with this weak Sunday-morning Laodiceanism that it would be a sensation indeed.

We glory these days in our churches being precise. Every "i" is dotted, every "t" is crossed. We are disciples of the great happy medium. Now, because there are extremes, our Lord would not have us be middle-of-the-roaders. He said he would spew us out of his mouth, not for being too hot, but for being lukewarm. He would rather have us on the wrong side of the fence than on the fence. Yet today the churches are on the fence. We do not commit ourselves boldly to anything. We are so cautious that half of what we say cancels the other half and we end up by having said nothing. We are salt without savor; there is no tang, no flavor, no relish about us, nothing to smack the lips over. Our services are dry and flat and tasteless, and when we try to pep them up with a little glorified "spizzerenctum" the result is embarrassing. We need a New Testament sensation-ism—not an emotional spree but the earth-shaking stir of a movement of the Holy Spirit. To have that, we need only to be New Testament Christians, when things will begin to happen. The most sensational thing I can imagine would be an outbreak of New Testament Christianity. It would create a sensation among the churches, for it would be a revival, an awaking out of sleep. Some churches have slept so long that the awakening would be as remarkable as Rip Van Winkle's. It would certainly create a sensation in this world, for the world has become so accustomed to our being comfortably hidden away in brick buildings on street corners that if a revival drove us out as at Pentecost to declare in the marketplaces the wonderful works of God, the general public would gather amazed, confounded, perplexed.

I am not advocating mere noise and uproar, but the Acts of the Apostles is an exciting book. And most of the denominations that now repose in such quiet dignity had a rather stirring start. The Baptists have subsided until one would hardly think that they were once considered heretical nuisances, so greatly did they disturb the peace. Surely the Methodists have a name for setting the woods on fire in days gone by. And even the Presbyterians, long synonymous with dignity, were once agitators second to none. Some of our denominationalists who fear that a holy stir in the house of God would be out of keeping with their tradition need to learn that it would be entirely in keeping—they would merely be returning to what they started with! If any of our modern denominations had started with no more zeal than they now have, they wouldn't be living today to tell the tale!

Intolerant, unpopular, sensational—such was the New Testament church. And so will we be if we dare to follow in that train. What kind of people were these New Testament Christians? They believed in Jesus Christ as Savior and Lord. They did not live on a memory; they believed in One who had died, had risen, and was coming again. They were filled with the Spirit. They were living a supernatural life in this present world. They were all witnesses. To them a missionary was not somebody to visit the church now and then to talk about Africa or China. Every Christian was a missionary.

Let us try that today, and something will happen. Personal faith in a risen, coming Christ. The infilling of the Spirit, our duty and privilege, as we yield all, receive, trust, and obey. The daily practise of Galatians 2:20, living by the faith of the Son of God. Every Christian a missionary. Let a few in any church start living that, and the impact will shake the community. For that is the way it started.

# CHAPTER 11

# Doing Something About It

*"They hear thy words but they will not do them" (Ezekiel 33:31).*

*"But be ye doers of the word, and not hearers only, deceiving your own selves" (James 1:22).*

The prophet Ezekiel ministered in an evil time. It was his lot to prophesy to a generation that listened after a fashion, likened him unto one having a pleasant voice, told others about his preaching, but did nothing about his message. They heard his words but did them not.

Ezekiel was not the only man of God whose sermons fell on unresponsive ears. Earlier, God had advised Isaiah well in advance that his message would blind eyes and shut ears and harden hearts lest the hearers convert and be healed. And those words show up later in each of the four Gospels and still later in Acts and Romans to explain the poor response of Israel to the ministry of our Lord and of Paul. Israel heard but did nothing.

James warns against the same evil. Invariably we do not quote the entire verse. We say, "But be ye doers of the word, and not hearers only," and there we stop. But there is a most solemn further word: "deceiving your own selves." That is the worst thing about it: hearing and not doing, we delude ourselves.

Our Lord constantly warned against doing nothing about it. "Everyone that heareth these sayings of mine and doeth them not, shall be likened unto a foolish man, which built his house upon the sand." "If ye know these things, happy are ye if ye do them." "Ye are my friends, if ye do whatsoever I command you." "Why call ye me Lord, Lord, and do not the things which I say?"

In the Great Commission, we are told to go "teaching them TO OBSERVE" the things commanded.

Chief among the besetting sins of the saints is hearing without doing. And it is a grievous sin, for "to him that knoweth to do good and doeth it not, to him it is sin." In Ezekiel's day they heard the preacher, complimented him, told others about him, but did nothing about the message. The centuries have passed, and today we listen to preachers, invite others to hear them, congratulate them with that very doubtful compliment, "I enjoyed your sermon." But we do nothing about it.

Let it never be forgotten that, although we may do nothing about the Word we hear, the Word will do something to us. The same sun melts ice and hardens clay, and the Word of God humbles or hardens the human heart. Truth heard and not acted upon is a dangerous thing. Spiritual impulses which are not translated into action have a disastrous reaction.

It is well known that many movie-goers who are continually being excited and stirred in the world of make-believe become emotional drunkards. But there are also religious drunkards and Bible-conference drunkards and church drunkards, who go from meeting to meeting, constantly being stirred but doing nothing about it, until their souls become fed-up, their moral muscles deteriorate, and they lose their capacity for being aroused. Presently they suffer from a moral let-down, a religious hangover. They delude themselves. They have heard the best preachers, they have read the best books, they have had their ears tickled and their emotions thrilled; but as with a stimulant, the doses have to be increased and after awhile there is no effect, no matter what they read or hear. An alarm clock that fairly blasts us out of bed on the first morning may eventually fail to arouse us if we continually ignore it. Something like that happens to those who hear and do not.

It is a serious thing to trifle with any emotion and not carry it through to its proper and legitimate conclusion. And it is most dangerous to play with the holy stirrings of God's Spirit through his Word. I had rather take chances with forked lightning any time. For the Word of God is dynamite, it is a hammer, a fire, a sword; messengers of the Word are a savor of life unto life and of death unto death. The man who habitually hears the Word of God and does nothing about it is the greatest of fools, for he fools himself.

Americans are a generation of spectators. They sit, thousands strong, in a football stadium and watch twenty-two men strive for the mastery down below. Then they go to the movies and thrill to the sham of Hollywood. On Sunday some of them go to church, and once again they are spectators before whom the minister is expected to perform. Many of them have no more intention of doing anything about the sermon than they intend to act out the movies. They are spectators, not participants.

Modern Christians find it easy to hear the Word and do nothing about it. Preaching may be had on every hand—at church, at the turn of a radio dial. Sermons have become so commonplace that we take the truth for granted. But where much has been given, much shall be required. God forbid that we should go out of our churches merely comparing one minister with another, like the listeners of Ezekiel's day, complimenting the messenger without conforming to the message, passing it up as just another sermon, "enjoying" it when God meant that our consciences should be pricked by it. The task of the preacher is "to comfort the afflicted and afflict the comfortable," and we are comfortable enough. God help us if we let the fowls of the air snatch up the seed which should produce thirty, sixty, an hundredfold; if we behold ourselves in the mirror of the Word and straightway forget what manner of persons we are!

The great and holy themes of Scripture are always joined with a call to do something about it. The first part of Ephesians shows us our exalted position in Christ, but right out of those heavenly glories we move from doctrine to duty, to the believer's vocation, which too often is regarded as a vacation. There are those who enjoy a dissertation on "The Lord knoweth them that are his" but who resent an application of the rest of the verse, "and let every one that nameth the name of Christ depart from iniquity."

It is possible to revel in prophetic lectures, "seeing that all these things shall be dissolved," without going on to do something about what manner of persons we ought to be. The coming of our Lord is a certainty, a coming certainty, a comforting certainty, and a challenging certainty, and if we hold properly this hope we shall do something about it, we shall purify ourselves even as he is pure. Alas, it is too often the case that the same brother who shouts "amen"—and well he may!—through the fifteenth chapter of First Corinthians, the resurrection chapter, shuts his mouth as tightly as his pocketbook on the sixteenth chapter, the collection chapter!

From start to finish, the Word of God joins creed with deed, and if "cursed be he that handleth the word of God deceitfully," let us remember that one way we can do that is by hearing it and not doing it. "Sin will keep us from the Book and the Book will keep us from sin," and it is not the Word hidden in the head but in the heart that keeps us from sin. You can have a head full of Scripture and a heart full of sin! You can backslide with a Bible under your arm!

It is possible to mistake a familiarity with Bible terms for a knowledge of Bible truth. We are not suffering from a lack of sermons. Maybe we have too many sermons. There is enough of the Word of God stored in the heads of Christians, if it were obeyed, to set America on fire and set off enough divine power to put atomic bombs to shame in comparison.

But something has to be done about the Word. It is true, gloriously true, that God's Word will not return unto him void. Ezekiel was assured that although the people would not heed his message, they would know that a prophet had been among them. Many a preacher, in an unresponsive day, has encouraged himself with that blessed truth. But that God's Word will not return void is no lollipop to roll under our tongues while we evade personal responsibility. The preacher has a responsibility to preach the Word, but his hearers have a responsibility to heed it. There is another verse about the Word not profiting Israel long ago, "not being mixed with faith in them that heard it." There must be a volitional response, "faith taking hold of the word."

We may have faith, but is it OBEDIENT faith? "By faith Abraham OBEYED." Are you obedient to the truth you know? Let me confine myself to the book of James and ask you a few pointed questions from that brief letter whence came our text about being doers of the Word and not hearers only, deceiving our own selves. And don't put these verses in a dispensational cubbyhole, they are for us all!

"Draw nigh to God and he will draw nigh to you. Cleanse your hands, ye sinners; and purify your hearts, ye double minded." This is to Christians. Have you done anything about that lately?

"Ye ask and receive not, because ye ask amiss, that ye may consume it upon your lusts." Have your prayers been unanswered because of sin?

"Let every man be slow to hear, slow to speak, slow to wrath." Have you done anything about your tongue and temper lately?

"Humble yourselves in the sight of the Lord, and he shall lift you up." Have you been proud? We want to have a revival and still save our faces, but the first thing we lose in a revival is our face!

"Speak not evil one of another, brethren.... Confess your faults one to another, and pray one for another, that ye may be healed." Are you critical? Is there someone to whom you owe an apology?

These are only a few verses, chosen almost at random. Think what would happen if the church did something about one little book, the book of James!

God help us to do something about it, lest we hear God's words and do them not, deceiving our own selves. "If ye know these things, happy are ye if ye do them."

CHAPTER 12

# We Still Have Jesus

*"And when they had lifted up their eyes, they saw no man, save Jesus only" (Matthew 17:8).*

Peter wanted to build three tabernacles to house his mountain-top experience. That didn't work, but when the glorious experience had passed he still had Jesus.

I remember how, years ago, I felt that I needed a deeper experience. I was growing dull and stale. I left my church for a few days and took a train for a little town deep in the Blue Ridge Mountains. There I nearly exhausted myself climbing a high peak, and spent an afternoon praying in a deserted schoolhouse. But I didn't find my "experience," and came back rather crestfallen.

Sometime later I had the same impulse again. Away I went in the springtime to my old home in the hills. I set out one sunny morning for my hide-out in the woods. The stage was set, as it were, and I felt that if I could get into the right mood I would get the fresh touch from heaven that I needed. But, try as I would, nothing came of it. I sat half-asleep, smitten with spring fever, and listened to the birds in the treetops. I finally stole out of the woods in low spirits, feeling more stupid than ever.

Again, down in Florida one winter, vacationing among the orange groves, I felt the same urge again. I took long walks beside the lake and sought to stir up the dormant fires within me. Nature and the weather certainly cooperated. But I was tired from months of preaching, and the exalted frame of mind just wouldn't come. One afternoon, as I strolled along the water's edge, I found myself repeating a poem I had learned years before:

We cannot kindle when we will
The fire which in the heart resides;
The Spirit bloweth and is still,
In mystery our soul abides.
But tasks in hours of insight willed
Can be in hours of gloom fulfilled.

I thought of Jesus' word about the wind blowing "where it listeth" and how we cannot trace the movements of God's Spirit nor regulate and produce them as we will. I thought of Peter and how he wanted to keep the experience when he had something better—he had Jesus. And then and there I rejoiced that although experiences come and go, I always have Jesus, the same yesterday and today and forever. "When darkness veils his lovely face, I rest on his unchanging grace." Everything else may come and go, all else may fail, all else may change, but we still have Jesus.

I rejoice that God has not seen fit to give me a dazzling experience. If he had, I might have talked about it and then people might have tried to have the same experience and, failing, they might have grown discouraged. But I have Jesus and I can always leave them with him and know that "heaven and earth may pass away, but Jesus never fails."

It is easy to be a Thomas and demand some rare experience, forgetting that Jesus said, "Blessed are they that have not seen and yet have believed." Most people live by "dry faith" anyway, and one can be a greater blessing if he lives by simple trust in him whom having not seen he loves than if he were forever relating mountain-top thrills and mystic visions.

I am not discrediting your colorful experience if you really had one. It is so easy to dramatize and glamorize such things. I have attended ministers' meetings where a brother could report receiving two new members into his church in such a way that you would think a new Jonah had risen and converted his Nineveh. But you cannot over-magnify Jesus; and when you are occupied with him, you are always on safe ground. You never lie awake nights regretting what you said when you brag on Jesus.

I used to become almost vexed trying to make the saints over. Some of them can be notoriously stubborn, and then we preachers want to skin them alive. Oh, we call it righteous indignation, of course, but that isn't what it is. Eventually we learn—or we should learn—that he is the center, and when we preach him we never get off center.

One can understand the Dutchman who grew weary of so much doctrinal controversy and said he "sure would like to get into a good old Jesus meeting." When Moody went to Scotland the church was in a poor way. There had been the Disruption thirty years earlier, and now the Free Church had sunk into formalism. Liberal teaching from Germany had crept in. It was a crisis, and Moody, knowing nothing of all this, came along, not as an expert to settle their troubles, for then he would have settled nothing. He came preaching Christ and him crucified, and it was said, "It seemed as though someone set to music the tune which had been haunting thousands of ears."

That is the note we need to hear. We need a revival, but we shall never have it by listening to lectures on revival. A revival is the church falling in love with Jesus Christ all over again. We are in love with ourselves, in love with our particular crowd, in love with our fundamentalism, maybe, but not in love with him.

We need to get back to him. Whatever else fails, we always have Jesus. Sometimes health fails, but we can take it to him and say, "He whom thou lovest is sick." Some turn to the Great Physician and are healed. Some are not. But in either case, "whether we live, we live unto the Lord; or whether we die, we die unto the Lord." We still have Jesus!

Sometimes our feelings fail us. John the Baptist, rugged preacher of the wilderness, folded up in prison, even as you and I. He became uneasy about Jesus, but Jesus hadn't failed. He was running on schedule. The disciples on the stormy sea saw the Lord and thought he was an apparition. They saw a ghost when they should have seen him. We have our ghosts, our bugaboos, our hobgoblins. A hillbilly discovered one midnight that he was in a graveyard. He got out in record time, fell over several tombstones, scratched himself tearing through the bushes. Next morning someone asked him, "Don't you know a ghost can't hurt you?" "I know that," he replied, "but they can make you hurt yourself." Our imaginary fears can indeed do that and fear has been called "the dark room where human negatives are made." The cure for fear is Jesus: "Be of good cheer; it is I; be not afraid."

Sometimes friends fail us. The psalmist lamented that his own familiar friend, in whom he trusted, who did eat of his bread, had lifted up his heel against him. Paul declared that no man stood with him in his hour of trial, but he went on to add, "Notwithstanding the Lord stood with me." He still had Jesus!

When loved ones are taken, Christ remains. There is a precious word in the account of the death and burial of John the Baptist: "And his disciples came, and took up the body, and buried it, AND WENT AND TOLD JESUS." After you have buried your John, you still have Jesus!

Sometimes the church fails. The true church shall not fail, for the gates of hell shall not prevail against it. But the professing church fails so often to rise to its opportunity. When the disciples failed to cast the demons out of the boy at the foot of the Mount of Transfiguration Jesus had not failed. He said, "Bring him to me." The church faces a demonized world today and, alas, it must often be said of us, "And they could not." Silver and gold we have but we are not saying, "Rise and walk." Peter, who once had asked, "What shall we have?" could say to the cripple at the Beautiful Gate, "Such as I have I give." The church today reverses the process, and instead of considering what we can give, we ask, "What do I get?" We are riddled with divisions, and much of our activity defeats itself. We are powerless before a needy world, but Christ has not failed. Let us bring men to him. His touch still has its ancient power. We still have Jesus!

When we look out upon the world we see certainly it has failed. We see not yet all things put under him but we see Jesus. There is so much that "we see not yet." "Change and decay in all around we see," but Christ changes not—he abides. And he is still accessible. It was a devout Christian doctor who once said in quiet conversation with a great preacher, "What the world needs is an emperor, and his name is Jesus Christ." Well, the world does need a king and one day Jesus shall reign. Men cannot master the world's problems. After the First World War it was the Big Four. After the Second it was the Big Three. But our troubles will not be over until there is only One, the King of kings and Lord of lords.

If you are unsaved, whatever else you may have tried, there is still Jesus. He stands at your heart's door and, if you will open the door, he will come in and abide. Then you can say, "Whatever comes, whatever goes, I still have Jesus!"

> I've tried in vain a thousand ways
> My fears to quell, my hopes to raise;
> But what I need, the Bible says,
> Is ever only Jesus.

# CHAPTER 13

# This Is That

*"What meaneth this?" (Acts 2:12).*

*"This is that" (Acts 2:16).*

*"What shall we do?" (Acts 2:37).*

It was Sunday morning in the little village where I was vacationing. I attended the local church, the usual morning service typical of most village church services over the land. I sat, a stranger in the congregation, and looked over the gathering. I could pick out the deacons. The people were respectful and listened fairly well to the earnest young preacher. They were not particularly stirred but they did not go to sleep. Presently everybody left the church with a comfortable sense of having done their duty.

I could not help reflecting, as I sat in that meeting: "If we really believed the glorious things this preacher is talking about, these stupendous truths we have gathered here to perpetuate, would we sit so listlessly and go out so lifelessly? After all, if two thousand years ago there lived on this earth a Man who was also God, if he was all he claimed to be and if he did all the record says he did, we ought to be excited about it!"

What shall we do to recover the lost radiance of the Christian faith? Strange thing about us Christians: we would not leave our faith for anything, but neither will we live it! We would not give it up, but neither do we give it out. "Man has never been willing to give up the next world for this or this world for the next." We are afraid not to give something to the cause of Christ: we are equally afraid to give it everything. And yet, if it is worth anything it is worth everything. Who will arise in all the babel of our confusion, the rattle of our empty worship, the whir of our religious wheels-within-wheels, and recapture the fervor of the first apostleship? We shall have a dull time of it until we either live our faith or take down our sign.

The study of the Acts of the Apostles is always a delightful experience, for something was happening every minute in those days. It can be a disturbing experience, for it shows us up in all our complacency and coldness. And it can be a depressing experience, for when one compares the flaming fervor of the first church with the pitiful imitation we behold today it is evident that a lot of water has run under the bridge since those days.

Human nature has not changed; the human heart is the same. The early church met about the same kinds of problems we face today, the same combinations of opportunity and opposition, "open doors and many adversaries." They wore different clothes and were called by different names, but essentially the same issues were involved. But then the church was in conflict with the forces without; now she is at a compromise with them. Then it was antagonism: now it is often alliance.

The early church met Sadduceeism. The Sadducees denied the resurrection—they were rationalists. We call them modernists—a misnomer, for modernism is not modern; it is one of the mustiest things in existence. We have had it ever since men first doubted God's Word and denied the supernatural. But the church today is not meeting Sadduceeism as the early church met it. Then it was outside the church; now it is inside, even in pulpits, where we are told that the Bible merely contains God's Word. Bob Ingersoll was an agnostic, but he was honest enough to stay out of the pulpit. Not all of his successors have shown that much consistency.

The early church met pharisaism. That was ritualism, form without force. Once again, what was outside the church then is inside now. And do not think that "having a form of godliness but denying the power thereof" applies only to liberal churches. There are fundamental fellowships, right in their dispensations and wrong in their dispositions, resting at ease in Zion, snug and smug in their orthodoxy, but just as powerless in their holier-than-thou pharisaism as the groups they censure.

The early church encountered Ananias and Sapphira. Their sin did not lie in giving part or in keeping part but in pretending that the part was the whole. The church was at such a fever heat of consecration that liars could not stand it. If we had spiritual purity like that in our sanctuaries there would be corpses all over the place. But today, men with fingers crossed, one hand behind their backs, sing, "I surrender all." Although we have had courses galore in stewardship and have been told countless times that we are not our own but are bought with a price, we still withhold from God our time and talents and money and, above all, ourselves. We are not in contrast with Ananias and Sapphira but in collusion with them!

The early church met persecution. Peter and John were forbidden to preach in the name of Jesus. But instead of praying for diplomacy, the church prayed for more boldness—the thing that got them into trouble in the first place. From then on, the path of the church was a path of blood and fire; but "the blood of the martyrs was the seed of the church." The church always has prospered in persecution but suffered in prosperity. She is "secure in danger but endangered by security." She has always been rich when poor, and poor when rich. She has had least treasure in heaven when she has had most money in the bank. You cannot stop the church by persecution: cut off one head and two more will appear. But if you want to smother the church patronize and popularize her. Fill her rolls with the worthless names of unregenerate members. Fill her offices with unconsecrated worldlings, her choirs with unsaved singers, her societies with social climbers, and you will discover that what Satan could never accomplish as a roaring lion of persecution he can achieve as a patronizing angel of light.

The early church met idolatry. I am thinking of Paul in Athens. He did not come to Athens as a tourist but as an evangelist, and as he walked in that center of art and culture he saw only their need of Christ. It has been said that "the ugly little Jew had no eye for beauty," but he did have. He had seen Jesus, and it had utterly spoiled him for everything else.

"He had seen the face of Jesus, tell him not of aught beside; He had seen the face of Jesus and his soul was satisfied."

In Athens Paul saw only a city given to idolatry. He did not sit around discussing the favorite subjects of those Athenians forever chasing some new thing. He had only one subject and he lost no time getting around to it. They listened until he came to the resurrection and repentance, and then, like many in the twentieth century, they smiled him away. Today they tell us preachers that when we go to Athens we should read up on their favorite subjects, and we have done so. Instead of meeting the intellectualism of the age with the resurrection and a call to repentance, we have gone in for book reviewing. We have joined the clubs of Athens; we have attended her pink teas and laughed at her jokes. We have modeled our sermons to tickle her ears. (For further information read the sermon subjects in Saturday newspapers!)

Paul left Athens, never to return. He went back to places where he was persecuted, but he had no time to waste on that mild, intellectual curiosity which we court so fervently today.

The early church met demonism, in Philippi and Ephesus, for instance. Paul, as usual, had a head-on collision. If you think our cities are any better today, you don't know our cities. Never was demonism more rampant. Walk up and down the streets; listen to the hellish jungle music floating from every haunt of sin. Listen to the foul blasphemy that fills the polluted air. Read the hideous crimes in our newspapers. If you are honest you will conclude that demonism is no outmoded superstition of an ignorant past. But the church today is not meeting it as Paul met it; she is trying to handle it with psychiatry instead of preaching. She has forgotten that only when the Stronger Man has bound the strong man can we say: "Greater is he that is in me than he that is in the world."

The early church met Apollos. A learned man, a disciple of John the Baptist, he was living up to the light he had. He did not know the full truth of the gospel or the power of the Spirit until he sat the feet of Aquila and Priscilla. Sometimes there are preachers who need to sit at the feet of some of their own congregation, as Apollos sat here and as Moody sat centuries later, to learn the deeper lesson of the enduement from on high. And there are many churches no farther along than Apollos. There are congregations of whom it might truly be said, so far as experience is concerned, "We have not so much as heard whether there be any Holy Ghost."

No matter what the early church met, she met it triumphantly. What is the matter with us that we do not follow in her train? What shall we do to recapture the lost radiance? We are up to our ears in problems, and we generally end up our discussions by saying, "And there's nothing you can do about it." Is there nothing we can do about it? Are we to accept conditions as they are, fold our hands, and say, "Let well enough alone; things could be worse"?

There was a reason for the radiance of the early church, and that reason was Pentecost. Two questions were asked by the people who looked on that day: "What meaneth this?" and "What shall we do?" Today we are trying to reverse the order. We are trying to make men ask, "What must I do to be saved?" before they have seen enough in our churches to make them inquire: "What meaneth this?" We are emphasizing evangelism without revival, which is not God's order. When men first have been amazed by a church filled with the Spirit we may expect them to inquire further as to the way of salvation.

"What meaneth this?" they asked. Peter said, "This is that which was spoken by the prophet Joel." Now, there is more in the prophecy of Joel than this quotation that may be applied to our profit today. Joel lived in a day of trouble, of calamity and judgment. We live in a day of judgment which has begun at the house of God, corrective judgment for the saint and condemnatory judgment for the sinner.

Joel was a revivalist. He called first for A SWEEPING REVIVAL. It was a call to all ages: "Gather the people, sanctify the congregation, assemble the elders, gather the children, and those that suck the breasts: let the bridegroom go forth of his chamber and the bride out of her closet." A revival may be spear-headed by youth, for example; but to be a real revival it must reach all ages. Middle-aged people are too inclined to sit back and let the young people go forward. We are told in Acts that the man who was healed was over forty years of age. When any-thing phenomenal happens to the forty-year-olds these days it is worthy of special mention. Preachers were included in Joel's call: "Let the priests, the ministers of the Lord, weep...." What is needed today is a stirring of God's Spirit among all ages, all groups, in pulpit and pew.

Joel called also for A WEEPING REVIVAL: "Gird your-selves and lament, ye priests: howl, ye ministers of the altar: come, lie all night in sackcloth, ye ministers of my God.... Sanc-tify ye a fast, call a solemn meeting, gather the elders and all the inhabitants of the land into the house of the Lord your God, and cry unto the Lord." It reminds us of James: "Be afflicted and mourn and weep: let your laughter be turned to mourning and your joy to heaviness." Mr. Finney used to say there could be no revival until Mr. Amen and Mr. Wet-Eyes could be found in the congregation.

David tells us that what God wants is a broken and contrite heart. Nehemiah wept. Paul warned men night and day with tears. Jesus wept. The Spirit prays for us with unutterable groan-ings. We had better groan a little for ourselves!

Joel gives us the proper motive for revival. The ministers were to pray: "Spare thy people, O Lord, and give not thine heritage to reproach, that the heathen should rule over [or use a by-word against] them: wherefore should they say among the people, Where is their God?" Men are bypassing the church today and saying in derision, "Where is your power? Where is the Holy Spirit you talk about? You have nothing from heaven." Why do we want revivals? Preachers sometimes want them in order to enhance their reputations. Churches want them in order to increase their membership. Sometimes we want our loved ones saved so that they will be easier to live with. All this is selfish. We are not to want revival primarily for the world's sake or America's sake or even the churches' sake but for God's sake, for the honor of his name, that the world may no longer pass by and jeer. "Not unto us, O Lord, not unto us but unto thy name give glory for thy mercy and for thy truth's sake. Wherefore should the heathen say, Where is now their God?"

Then Joel pleads for A REAPING REVIVAL, and there will always be a harvest, both material and spiritual. "Then will the Lord be jealous for his land and pity his people." Has God not told us that if his people repent he will forgive and heal the land? Joel says he will send corn and wine and oil. Under grace as well as then there are physical by-products in a genuine revival. God will restore the years the locust hath eaten, says Joel, and he has done just that again and again. And there will be the pouring out of his Spirit as there was at Pentecost and as there may be in gracious infillings when the church turns to the Lord. Notice that just as all ages were invited by Joel to repent, so all ages share in the blessing. The Spirit is to be poured out on all flesh: sons and daughters shall prophesy, old men shall dream dreams, and young men see visions; servants and handmaidens shall receive the Spirit. And there will be the reaping of souls, for whoever shall call upon the name of the Lord shall be saved. After the church has her lost joy restored and is upheld afresh by the Spirit, transgressors will be taught God's ways and sinners be converted.

The church will not get on its feet until it first gets on its knees. Ezekiel said, "The Spirit entered into me and set me upon my feet." After we have repented and are Spirit-filled, we shall stand on our feet in testimony and men shall first ask, "What meaneth this?" and then, "What shall we do?"

CHAPTER 14

# Sunrise Tomorrow

There has always been a peculiar charm about sunrise. It has been the theme of many popular songs like "The World Is Waiting tor the Sunrise" and that wedding favorite, "At Dawning." Poems aplenty have been written about sunsets, but there is a different beauty that belongs to sunrise. Probably not many of us see enough sunrises to enter into their secrets. I am not parading myself as an early riser. I miss more sunrises than I see. But some that I have seen will abide in my heart forever. There is something about darkness giving way to light, the mystery of a new day being born, the eastern sky aflush and then aflame, that lingers in the soul.

Sick people can tell us much about sunrise, for they have passed many a restless night longing for the break of day. They know what the psalmist meant when he said, "My soul waiteth for the Lord more than they that watch for the morning: I say, more than they that watch for the morning." They understand Job when he said: "When I lie down, I say, When shall I arise and the night be gone? and I am full of tossings to and fro unto the dawning of the day."

I remember such a night years ago when I was suffering from nervous exhaustion and was unable to sleep. I spent the night in a cottage beside a lovely lake. I was to preach next day in a city church nearby, and I needed a good night's rest but could not obtain it. Of course, the harder one tries to sleep, the less likely he is to succeed. Toward morning, I gave up and resigned myself to watching for the day. I remember the first faint intimation of coming light. I could not put my finger on the clock at any one minute and say, "Here began the day." But there was the gentle,

93

gradual fading of the darkness; a few birds chirped in the trees; there was soon a glint on the water; by and by, the first rosy tint flushed the east; and through it all grew the mystery of the world waiting for the sunrise.

One who has passed sleepless morning hours may learn to "meditate in the night watches," to pray if he cannot sleep. He begins to understand why the saintly fathers rose early for a session with God. He knows why the New England Pilgrims prayed at sunrise. Bradford tells of an Indian attack at daybreak while they were so engaged. He recalls William Law and that he rose at five because he was a Christian and, when tempted to stay in bed, reminded himself, "I am an old man and am far behind with my sanctification." So he flung himself out of bed before the servants had made their fires or the farmers had yoked their horses, for he thought it a shame to lie folded up in bed when life was so short and there was so much to do.

Again, one thinks of Jacob wrestling with the angel and crossing Peniel at sunrise, limping but having power with God and men. Especially does one think of the Savior, who, "rising up a great while before day, went out and departed into a solitary place and there prayed." Evidently he found it good to wait on God while the world was waiting for the sunrise.

We are told that during Paul's experience in the storm at sea "they cast out four anchors and wished for the day." We are passing through one of the worst moral and spiritual hurricanes in history; multitudes are at sea, and many are wishing for the day. Whether on beds of pain or bowed down with sorrow or burdened with the uncertainty of today and dread of tomorrow, millions were never so weary of the night and so anxious for the day. And never have so many been homesick for heaven. They have cast their anchor safe and sure and are waiting till the day dawns and the shadows flee away. "Weeping may endure for a night, but joy cometh in the morning."

But so many dear souls are not sure about the sunrise. There is small comfort in a vague hope that "everything will turn out all right." There is little solace in a mere Pollyanna optimism and a

Micawberish philosophy that "something will turn up." Nor will Utopian dreams of a better world, a brotherhood of man welded together by politicians and diplomats, satisfy the soul.

In the account of one of the appearances of our risen Lord, it is stated: "When the morning was come, Jesus stood on the shore." The Christian is looking for morning. For him "the morning cometh." But to him sunrise means Son-rise, it is the Son that brings the morning. "To depart and be with Christ" is daybreak for the saint. Then he says good night here and good morning up there.

But I am thinking of another sunrise that is due some tomorrow. It is the sunrise the Savior promised when he said, "I will come again." It is the sunrise promised at his ascension: "This same Jesus shall so come in like manner as ye have seen him go away." It is the sunrise Paul promised when he wrote, "The Lord himself shall descend from heaven with a shout, with the voice of the archangel and with the trump of God." It is the sunrise Peter promised when he said, "The chief shepherd shall appear." It is the sunrise promised by John when he wrote: "When he shall appear we shall be like him, for we shall see him as he is." Christ is both Son and Sun, both Son of God and Sun of Righteousness, of whom it was said that he should arise with healing in his wings. He was called the Dayspring from on high, and Peter tells us to take heed unto prophecy until the day dawn and the Daystar arise in our hearts. For the Son-rise, for the return of Christ the world is waiting. Ruined by sin, it has never been happy and never will be until he shall reign whose right it is.

THE PHYSICAL WORLD IS WAITING FOR THE SUNRISE. "For the earnest expectation of the creature [or creation] waiteth for the manifestation of the sons of God. For the creature was made subject to vanity, not willingly, but by reason of him who hath subjected the same in hope. Because the creature itself also shall be delivered from the bondage of corruption into the glorious liberty of the children of God. For we know that the whole creation groaneth and travaileth in pain together until now" (Rom. 8:19-22). This world of tooth and claw, of thorn and thistle, of sweat and blood, is a world that crashed because of sin. The animals that cringe in fear, the birds that furtively look around with every step they take, all proclaim a reign of terror that started with Adam and shall end when the Savior shall redeem the earth, when the lion and lamb shall lie down together. The Scriptures describe such a blessed state: "The wolf also shall dwell with the lamb, and the leopard shall lie down with the kid; and the calf and the young lion and the fatling together; and a little child shall lead them. And the cow and the bear shall feed; and their young ones shall lie down together: and the lion shall eat straw like the ox. And the sucking child shall play on the hole of the asp, and the weaned child shall put his hand on the cockatrice's den. They shall not hurt nor destroy in all my holy mountain: for the earth shall be full of the knowledge of the Lord, as the waters cover the sea" (Isa. 11:6-9). Here is a picture of a world which we have never seen but which we shall see after sunrise, when the night is past and the day has dawned.

THE POLITICAL WORLD IS WAITING FOR THE SUNRISE. The politicians do not know it, of course. They would try to make the day dawn by their efforts around conference tables. But the hope of a better day rests with only One, the Lord of glory. Only in Christ can you bring men together. Capital and labor have no trouble when they meet in the Lord. When Boaz saluted his laborers by saying, "The Lord be with you," and they answered, "The Lord bless thee," they gave us then and there the only solution of the labor problem. The white man and the black have no trouble when they both love the Lord. They have most trouble when starry-eyed idealists try to solve their problems. The rich man and the poor meet in Christ: there a Joseph of Arimathea stands on equal footing with fishermen-disciples. The learned and unlearned meet in Christ, and an uneducated D. L. Moody can work with renowned scholars and theologians bound by a common love. National lines melt in him with whom there is neither Jew nor Greek, bond nor free.

The scattered pieces of this bleeding world can never be put together by any conference of experts. Only the return of our

Lord holds the answer. There may be armistices and breathing spells while fresh confederacies form, but Christ alone will bring an end to dictators, just as he will bring an end to death and disease and depravity and the devil.

THE CHRISTIAN WORLD IS WAITING FOR THE SUNRISE. "And not only they [the creation], but ourselves also, which have the firstfruits of the Spirit, even we ourselves groan within ourselves, waiting for the adoption, to wit, the redemption of our body" (Rom. 8:23). The people of God are looking for the Lord. Certainly that was the New Testament attitude, not alone readiness but also expectancy, anticipation. They were not merely looking for something to happen, they were looking for Someone to come. "To wait for his Son from heaven"; "Unto them that look for him shall he appear"—that is the note of early Christianity. The Christian who understands his Bible is looking for the sunrise because he is looking for the Sun! Men may call him a pessimist, but he is looking for morning, not night. He has the brightest outlook of all, for he is looking for a day when there shall be no night. He has the happiest hope in all the world, for he anticipates a day when all tears shall be wiped from our eyes. He has the surest hope, for back of it is the authority of God's Word.

We are looking for Sunrise tomorrow. And it might be today! For indeed "the night is far spent, the day is at hand!"

# CHAPTER 15

# The Gait of Galilee

Jesus was an outdoor preacher. He knew about boats and fishing, flowers and birds, wind and weather, solitary places, growing grain, sunsets, and sheep and sparrows—the humble life of simple people. I am glad he didn't set up an office in Rome, Alexandria, Athens, or even Jerusalem. He spent his days in a tiny little Roman province, never went abroad, lectured in no universities. A country preacher, he traveled at a slow gait. In this modern bedlam with its heart attacks and nervous breakdowns, pep pills and tranquilizers, we desperately need to learn to live at his tempo—the gait of Galilee.

In spite of all of our time-saving devices, we do not have as much time as our forefathers. A friend of mine said recently: "When I was visiting in a neighboring town not long ago, an old gentleman asked me, 'Where do you live?' When I told him, he said, 'I used to come over there once in awhile in the horse-and-buggy days. It took a whole day then and now I can go in thirty minutes *but I don't have time."*

I grew up in the Carolina hills in the peaceful years just before 1914, when the world went crazy—and it has been insane ever since. This week in an old-fashioned South Carolina town I've been in the library perusing old copies of *The Literary Digest,* dated in the early 1900s. It is like slipping back into another world. The farmers of my boyhood days raised their cotton and ate their watermelons; they boiled their molasses and butchered their hogs; they went possum hunting and gathered at corn-shuckings and Sunday singings. They lived close to elemental things—sunrise and sunset, the pageant of the seasons, the joys and sorrows of birth and growth and marriage and old age. When life was over they were buried in the little country church graveyards. What most of them experienced cannot be sold in the market, it is true, but neither can it be bought there! That way of life is gone forever, along with the old parlor lamp and the fringe-topped surrey.

Recently a thunderstorm knocked out the electricity in our apartment, and, as I hunted for a candle, I couldn't help remembering the thunderstorms of my boyhood. Those storms created no problems. The milk would have been in the spring, the meat salted away, the old wood stove not affected by lightning, the kerosene lamp always ready. We didn't have television—for which let us be grateful!

In the summertime we had our revivals at "laying-by time," that lull between springtime and harvest. We met for morning services each day, ate dinner (not lunch) in each other's homes, then sat on the front porch and talked all afternoon. My father kept the preacher overnight when he came to preach every fourth Sunday. I was allowed to sit up late in the guest room to listen to Father and the minister talk long and late about the things of God.

There was time to live and to talk, then. Today, up and down that country road—now a highway—new houses stand. But the occupants are not farmers; they are commuters who work in town and ride back and forth in the rat race each day. Ear-splitting trucks roar through the hills. Even the preacher hurries in and out from Dan to Beersheba. If Jesus came to our Bethany today, Mary and Martha would be working in town. Or, if he did catch them at home, they wouldn't turn the TV down long enough to hear the Savior. Ask any pastor visiting his flock these days!

In the old days we lived miles apart but we were still neighbors. Now I live in a growing city and do not know anybody up and down my block. We are closer together than ever—yet farther apart.

The South, where I live, has become mechanized, industrialized, urbanized—and paganized. When we left the country for the city, somewhere on that journey we lost our souls.

The author of that charming "up-country memory," *Red Hills and Cotton,* tells how his grandfather was out of step with the shift from farm to factory. He feared that the new way of life would smother individuality and kill a man's inner glow. In the new era when men were awakened each morning by a whistle instead of by a rooster, he was afraid of the power of industry— the accumulation of wealth in the hands of a few. He believed that work should be a means to an end, with time at the close of the day to sit on the "piazza" and talk, and hours to walk alone in the fields and think.

As the Civil War ended, the northern armies invaded the South. Then came the industrial invasion and a new way of life. Charles and Mary Beard in *The Rise of American Civilization* called this industrial invasion a "second American Revolution." There were, of course, some scientific and material benefits; but we really gained a world and lost our souls. Something went out that will never come back. Lewis Mumford said, "The South will be wealthier in all things that money can buy and poorer in all the things that are beyond price or purchase."

Now all America, not only the South, having sown the wind is reaping the whirlwind. Experts gather in Washington to wrestle with the problem of urbanitis, crowded cities, the rush from the country to town. We laughed at farmers and called them hayseeds. Now we have a generation of city slickers and it is quite evident that "God made the country but man made the town." Nobody knows what to do with the madhouse we call Megalopolis with its garbage-can existence, its ghettos, its crime and filth and anarchy, its traffic congestion, poisoned air, polluted water, and ear-splitting noises.

Our Savior was not a city man. The reader of the Gospels, the traveler in Palestine, is impressed with the simplicity of his life on earth. Thirty years of quiet obscurity, three years of teaching by the sea or on the mountain or in little villages—we never would plan it that way. He was busy but never in a hurry. Today "progress" has invaded even the Holy Land. Countless shrines clutter the scene and commercialism sometimes spoils the day for those who would walk where Jesus walked. Blessed is the man, at home or abroad, who can manage somehow to recapture the gait of Galilee.

No one has time anymore for all the leisure that automation is supposed to give us. When have you seen anybody just walking and thinking? Along a highway these days such a curiosity would be judged either out of his head or out of gas.

What shall it profit us to gain the world of space travel, nuclear know-how, gadgets and gimmicks, if we lose our souls? The biggest joke of all is the illusion of progress. One civilization after another has started in hardship, grown rich and rotten, and perished—the victim of its own devices. America is no exception. We are a nation of sheep, the prisoners of our inventions, enslaved by the very system that was meant to set us free. We are unable to enjoy the leisure our machines have given us, because we are beggars without inner resources. I care not how big our houses are, how expensive our cars, how many stocks and bonds we have salted away; if in our souls we are paupers, we are already in the poor-house.

Recently I saw a beatnik ambling along with music (if you call *that* music) pouring from a transistor radio in his coat. Lacking a song in his heart, he carried it in his pocket!

Of course we can't go back to the old days. We are caught in the rat race and we're stuck with it. But unless we find time, or make time, for reflection and meditation, we shall be puppets on a string, cogs in a wheel, prisoners of our time. "The world is too much with us," said Wordsworth. "The journey is too great for thee" (1 Kings 19:7), said the angel to the tired Elijah. Like him, we are under the juniper and had better find a way to Horeb and the still, small voice.

In my first pastorate, a country charge in the Carolina lowlands, I spent much time with John Brown. He farmed back on a creek, a slow-moving man who thought and talked much about things that really mattered. I spent many an afternoon chatting with him when I should have been visiting my parishioners and he should have been plowing. The sinking sun would drive me home through the cypress swamp. Next day I would return and we never said, "Good morning," we just resumed our conversation where we had left off the day before. John Brown had time. He frequently came to my room of an evening to talk until midnight. Once we sat up all night with a sick man in the neighborhood. Nowadays we send such people to a hospital where they can pay a nurse to sit up. It has been thirty years since then and I have not found another man with that much time. Yet John Brown had only as many hours in the day as anyone else. He would have driven a go-getter, a driving businessman, crazy; but he was like the hillbilly who, when told he should get out into the world and make money so he could enjoy life, replied, "I'm enjoying it now!"

I must confess that I do not feel at home in the new South, the new America, the new age. They say that a man should not war with his time but the prophets did. As Paul Harvey says: "I didn't leave the old country, the old country left me." We haven't "seceded," the country has seceded from us. Some of us feel lonely as the new order moves on leaving us looking rather archaic. One of the outstanding Baptists of the last generation said: "I'm standing where Baptists used to stand. When they get right they'll be with me, for I'm where they used to be." I do not see any such return, either in state or church, but I feel no itch to ride the wave of the future. It is one way to get drowned.

It is almost impossible to find a spot of calm today. On my preaching trips I look for a patch of woods if the town is small, a park (a dangerous place to walk now) or a cemetery where at least nobody talks back. Our Lord rose a great while before day and departed to a solitary place to pray. He found time and place for communion with God and so must we, at any cost.

William Law asked, "Who am I to lie folded in a bed late of a morning when the farmers have already gone about their chores and I'm so far behind with my sanctification?" We are far behind with our sanctification these days, and one reason is that solitude is next to impossible and meditation is unheard of. When I take a walk nowadays, even the dogs look at me in wonderment—even to them a pedestrian is a novelty! A policeman spent some time recently watching a man out for a stroll—the very rareness of it excited suspicion!

There is a longing, a nostalgia, in the hearts of many for a return to the old pattern. We move into town to make enough money to buy a house back in the country! Our national parks are filled in the summertime. One look at the crowded tents and we see that the poor campers have brought along most of what they left home to get away from. This generation knows no privacy and it will get worse as the government snoops on us and home is no longer our castle.

We have paid a dear price for "progress." We have boxed ourselves in, and the dilemma is how to maintain our sanity in a madhouse where the inmates are trying to run the asylum.

For over fifty years in the ministry I have been a rebel in the rat race. I have never worked under orders from any headquarters but heaven. I have never filled out a blank reporting my activities to any swivel-chair overseer in an office. We have spurned the legacy of the prophet for the security of the priest. What the farmer lost when he went to the factory the prophet loses when he turns priest. The prophet faces the same problem as the independent grocer in a day of chain stores, or the little shopkeeper in a day of standardization, or the small farmer in a day of mass farm production. He is a Micaiah among the prophets of Ahab, an Amos at Bethel, a Daniel in the courts of Babylon. He follows the greatest Prophet of all who stood alone against the Pharisees. He bears the marks of his Master, not the number of antichrist. He belongs to nobody's little empire, pays tribute to no ecclesiastical monarch. He wears no buttons or badges and carries no banners for political projects disguised as moral issues. He runs his own shop in a day of religious big business, keeps his own store while the crowd flocks to the supermarkets, tends his own garden while his neighbors sell out to the cooperatives. In all this he walks in the footsteps of the greatest Prophet of all who set before us the proper pace for all who would walk as he walked—the gait of Galilee.

# Chapter 16

# Notes and Music

Some time ago I watched the great cellist, Pablo Casals, on television; he was teaching an advanced class of students. These young cellists were so good already that they did not seem to me to need any further instruction. But Casals did not feel that way. To one performer he said: *"You are playing the notes but not the music!"*

Something like that is the trouble with modern Christianity. We are playing the notes but not the music, singing the words but not the melody.

I remember a piano teacher of years ago. She was an excellent sight-reader. She could play any music set before her but it sounded mechanical and lifeless. I have heard better music played by untrained pianists who played by ear and couldn't read a note!

The Psalmist declared: "Thy statutes have been my songs in the house of my pilgrimage" (Psalms 119:54). Christians are strangers and pilgrims, exiles and aliens, passing the time of their sojourning in an unfriendly world. Matthew Henry said, "This world is our passage and not our portion." This world is not our rest. We have here no continuing city. This is the house of our pilgrimage.

While we make our way through these lowlands, we have a song. Some saints do more sighing than singing, but God has put a new song in our mouths and we ought to speak in psalms and hymns and spiritual songs, making melody in our hearts to the Lord. We are the melody makers!

What is our song? The Psalmist said, "Thy statutes have been my songs...." God's Word was his song. He did not just memorize or quote it, he sang it. We do not ordinarily associate statutes with songs, but God's lawbook is a songbook. His mandates are melodies, both words and music, both theology and doxology, both duty and delight.

The tragedy of the church today is that we are trying to have either the music without the notes or the notes without the music. Some would sing the tune without the words, as it were. They try to produce a Christian experience without Scripture or doctrine. I remember a meeting sponsored by a group that advocated beginning one's witnessing by telling one's experience – not by quoting Scripture. But "faith cometh by hearing, and hearing by the Word of God" (Romans 10:17). When we major in experience and leave the track of Scripture we are like a locomotive that has left the rails and is stuck in the mire with only the whistle blowing. It was after our Lord expounded the Scriptures to the Emmaus disciples that their hearts burned within them.

In the musical world our eardrums are battered by weird and wild discords that disregard every decent law of harmony. In the religious world we are seeing new varieties of so-called Christianity that deny the Scriptures and every doctrine of the faith. These "songs without words" range all the way from a jazz gospel at one extreme to a liberal social reform under religious auspices at the other. There is no redeeming message from God to men. It is only a pitiful effort at music without notes—songs without words.

But, as with Casal's cello student, it is possible to play the notes but not the music. After the service one Sunday morning, a great preacher asked a soloist who had displayed much art but not much heart, "Did you really mean those words or was it just a song?" How much of our worship these days needs to face that searching question!

The Pharisees were experts in the letter of the law but they knew not the spirit of it. There was no warmth, no heart, no joy in Pharisaism. What made other people happy made them miserable. What made others glad made them sad. When our Lord entered Jerusalem in triumph they said jealously, "... the world is gone after him." At the cleansing of the temple when the children were crying "Hosanna" and a revival was on, they inquired, "Hearest thou what these say?"

He had them in mind when, in the parable of the prodigal son, he pictured the pouting elder brother on the back porch irritated by the music and dancing. We have music and dancing aplenty these days, even in staid sanctuaries, what with jazz bands in church, gospel boogie on television, and church recreational buildings vibrating with religious hootenannies. But we are not rejoicing over prodigal sons come home to God, and if that kind of revival broke out, some prominent church members would become sulking Pharisees. Pharisaism plays the notes but not the music. It may be long on theology, but it is short on doxology. The score may be correct but the song is cold.

Evangelical Christianity today is occupied more with the notes than the music. I am disturbed by what I hear. I listen to learned discussion about relevance, dialogue, involvement. I watch panels, symposiums, seminars with intellectuals high in the theological stratosphere holding forth in terms unintelligible to men of low estate. My soul hungers like the Dutchman who asked, "Vot iss all dis argument? I sure vould like to get into another good old Jesus meeting!" We are all weary with lectures on music; what we need to hear is a song!

When Dwight L. Moody went to Scotland on his evangelistic mission, the churches were cold and divided after what was called "the Disruption." Mr. Moody probably knew nothing at all about that. He simply preached the grace of God and someone said: "It seemed as though someone had set to music a tune that had been haunting thousands of ears." Churchmen had argued about the notes but Moody played the music!

Something is missing today. This is not nostalgia for the good old days—some of the good old days weren't so good! It is not merely old age coming on, for many young preachers tell me they have the same concern and yearning as I. It is hard to describe. As the Scotsman said, it is easier felt than "telt." It is the first love that Ephesus had left and the joy of salvation that David had lost. It is that undefinable something that makes the difference. It does not always accompany pulpit fame or great learning. A PhD degree does not guarantee it. It is art without heart and light without heat. We come away from church hungry-hearted. The order of service was faultless. There was not one off note in the choir. The sermon was a model discourse. But it was a performance, not an experience. The minister may have been so polished that he sparkled, but while our eyes blinked at his brilliance, they did not fill with tears. We wondered whether it could be our own fault because sometimes it is the receiver that is to blame, not the transmitter! But we know that the coals in our heart still glow when the breath of the Spirit blows on them.

There are facts but not fire, notes but not music. Music is more than an assortment of notes. A love letter is more than a collection of nouns and verbs and adjectives. A sermon is more than thirty minutes' worth of homiletic material.

Nowadays, after I have read religious periodicals for a while, I have to stop to get the taste out of my mouth. Sometimes I play an album of sermons by George W. Truett. He was sound in his notes but his strongest point was in the music. I remember a great congregation moved to tears by one of his heart sermons. It was not a "tear jerker" either. He had what makes the difference.

Sometimes I play another record by the untrained choir of a great people's church. It is not a high-brow number and my existentialist friends would call it corny. It is about heaven and that is out of style, for who talks about going to heaven these days? But I sit there all alone and listen and have a one-man revival. As my old friend Homer Hammontree used to say, it makes me feel as though somebody had busted a jug of honey right in the middle of my soul.

I think of a Bible conference years ago where, in the dining room on the closing Sunday, somebody asked Lena, the negro cook, to sing for us. She stood in a corner, arms folded, and began the old spiritual, "Just A Closer Walk With Thee." Immediately I sensed the presence of the Spirit. Handkerchiefs came out all over the dining room; the fountains of the deep were broken up.

Many denominations were represented, but that day we were lifted above our fences. We might have argued about unification, but here was unity. Lena's song did not create it, it revealed it. She had struck the Great Common Denominator. We could all get together on that song. Lena ought to sing for all of our conferences and conventions. She probably didn't know a note in the book but she sang the music.

Of course, notes and music, words and tune, go together. There is no reason why one cannot have a head full of notes and a heart full of music. A great theologian can be a radiant Christian. A preacher can read from his Greek New Testament and still sing "The Old Time Religion."

Our big problem today, however, is akin to that of Casal's cello student. We are playing the notes, but somehow the music lacks a soul. We sing the words, but a song is not the sum total of words and tune. There is a third element, and if heart does not speak to heart it is but laryngeal sounds beating on eardrums. Place a Stradivarius in the hands of a Kreisler and the combination can lift one out of this world. Let any ordinary fiddler play it and you have only horsehair scraping on catgut.

Ephesus was busy with "works," but it was no longer "first works." The trouble was, she had left "first love." Only the love of God shed abroad by the Spirit can add the third ingredient. Then we make melody in our hearts and God's statutes become our songs in the house of our pilgrimage.

CHAPTER 17

# The Church Must First Repent

The message of John the Baptist was "Repent." Our Lord began his earthly ministry preaching "Repent." When his disciples started out on their first mission they preached repentance. Peter and Paul preached repentance. The last word of the Christ of Patmos to the Asian churches—and to us—was "Repent."

I have been preaching in churches for over half a century. I have read church bulletins galore announcing "revivals"; prescribing preparation for church in-gatherings; calling on the people to visit, invite, sing, and pray. All of this is good, but I have looked— almost in vain—for somebody to urge what is so obvious in the New Testament that only a blind spot in our eyes can account for our silence. Almost nothing is ever said about repentance: getting right with God and men, humbling ourselves, seeking God's face and turning from our wicked ways. We will do everything but repent. Of course, the average so-called "revival" is really just a drive for more church members, and the present fellowship is left untouched. We seem to assume that we are in good shape and that all we need to do is to move ahead from where we are. The status quo is not touched with a forty-foot pole. But the church is not ready to move ahead until she first repents. The status quo needs to be "un-quoed"!

Our Lord did not say to the church at Ephesus: "What you need is a bigger evangelistic program." He said, "Repent!" When Ephesus repents and regains her first love she will be evangelistic.

He did not say to Pergamos and Thyatira, "What you need is to step up your missionary activity." He said, "Repent!" When

111

churches repent and deal with Balaam and Jezebel they will be missionary churches.

He did not say to Sardis: "What you need is more tithers." He said, "Repent!" When Sardis repents she will be a generous church.

He did not say to Laodicea: "What you need is more witnessing laymen." When Laodicea moves from lukewarmness to boiling zeal, everybody will be a witness.

We do not make sick people well by telling them to act like well people. They are sick and the trouble must be dealt with first, then they will act like well people naturally. Getting church members to engage in religious activities before sin has been dealt with in their lives only compounds their trouble.

The issue is "Repent... or else." The alternatives to repentance as our Lord uttered them are severe: "I will remove... I will fight... I will kill... I will come as a thief... I will spew out of my mouth." On first reading these may not sound like Jesus but they are his words and they are the consequences that befall unrepentant churches.

Today cheap grace is being preached and received by cheap faith, resulting in cheap Christians. Even Dwight L. Moody preached repentance on his second evangelistic trip to Great Britain because "he had come to know that unless there was a genuine turning away from known sin in life and thought, there was little permanency of change."

Dr. Nelson Bell writes: "Repentance no longer seems a major concern of preaching or of the church. In fact, repentance in the biblical sense is almost a lost word even though it was central in the message of the early church."

The editor of *Watchman-Examiner* writes: "It is a word little used in fashionable religious circles. Most carefully cultured twentieth-century clergymen have dropped it from their vocabulary completely. Have you heard a sermon on repentance lately?"

On the Day of Pentecost Peter explained the mighty outpouring of the Spirit by saying, "But this is that which was spoken by the prophet Joel" (Acts 2:16). Read the prophet Joel and you will discover that he was a revivalist who called God's people to repentance: "Gird yourselves, and lament, ye priests: howl, ye ministers of the altar: come, lie all night in sackcloth, ye ministers of my God... turn ye even to me with all your heart, and with fasting, and with weeping, and with mourning... rend your heart, and not your garments" (1:13; 2:12-13). That is the language of repentance. Then follows the promise of the poured out Spirit, which is revival, and "whosoever shall call on the name of the Lord shall be delivered" (2:32). There is the conversion of the ungodly. It follows in logical order. We are having revolutions today—social, political, economic, scientific—but "this is not that." There is no spiritual revolution because the church has not repented. Some Christians get tangled up in these revolutions but only the impact of born-again, Bible-believing, Spirit-filled Christians will make any worthwhile difference today.

Repentance is not penance or penitence, but a change of mind about sin and self and God—a turning from sin and self to the Savior, being sorry enough for our sins to quit them. It means confession and cleansing and commitment. "He that covereth his sins shall not prosper: but whoso confesseth and forsaketh them shall have mercy" (Proverbs 28:13). Some are willing for God to take away their sins by forgiving them who are not willing to put away their sins by forsaking them. We must bring forth fruits meet for repentance, not just walk down a church aisle; we must prove we mean it by what we do afterwards.

Sam Jones said in one of his great meetings: "Until the church members of this city make restitution, confess slander, forgive one another, forsaking worldliness, social drinking, gambling and other sins, we are not ready to lead sinners to Christ. Let us clean up ourselves and sinners will be converted." That kind of preaching is out of style now for Joseph Parker said: "The man whose sermon is 'Repent' sets himself against this age and will for the time being be battered mercilessly by the age whose moral tone he challenges. There is but one end for such a man: 'Off with his head!' You had better not preach repentance unless you have pledged your head to heaven."

"Repent" is the first and last call of the New Testament. And except we repent, we shall all likewise perish.

Dr. B. H. Carroll said: "I give it as my deliberate conviction that the Christian profession of today owes its lack of vital godliness, its absence from prayer-meeting, its miserable semblance of missionary life very largely to the fact that old-fashioned repentance is so little preached. You can't put a big house on a little foundation."

The church must first repent. The majority of church members show little if any evidence of having been born again. If one is what he has always been he is not a Christian. I could have led some people to the Lord if they hadn't joined a church!

Too many are living in sin. The Christians in Corinth were proud of their tolerance of sin in their midst. The church at Thyatira "suffered"—put up with—Jezebel. Paul did not overlook the immoral brother in Corinth just because "they have a lot of good people." We are told today not to deal with sin in the church, just to preach love. Then why did Paul wait until the thirteenth chapter of his epistle to Corinth before he got around to love? There was sin in the church and it must be dealt with. He did not say, "Things could be worse," he believed things could be better and he would have them so!

Worldliness is rampant in the church. The devil is not fighting churches, he is joining them! He is not persecuting Christianity, he is professing it. What many think is the world becoming more Christian is Christians becoming more worldly. The friend of the world is the enemy of God, and if we love the world the love of the Father is not in us.

We are too proud. Jeremiah lamented: "Therefore the showers have been witholden, and there hath been no latter rain; and thou hadst a whore's forehead, thou refusedst to be ashamed" (3:3). We are not having revival showers because our hearts and our faces are hard toward God, like the face of a woman of the street.

There is no burden for a lost world. Americans spend more on dog food than they give to foreign missions.

In such a time preaching repentance is the loneliest and most thankless sort of ministry. People like to go to great religious gatherings where they can get lost in the crowd. But let a prophet stand in a local church and face a congregation where everybody knows everybody else and let him try to call deacons and choir singers and Sunday school teachers to get right with God, and he will get a chilly reception!

We are hearing these days that it is "evangelize or perish"; that there is widespread interest in religion but a revolt against the church; that a bridge must be built between the church and the world or little will be left of the church in a few years; that we must make better use of our laymen; that "the salt of the earth" must be shaken out of our million-dollar salt cellars—our magnificent sanctuaries—and rubbed into the putrefaction of modern society. To all this we agree. But the church must first repent, confess and forsake sin, get right with God and man, renounce the world, make Christ Lord, and be filled with the Spirit. Why is nothing said about this? We are not ready to evangelize until then. Laymen are not ready to witness until then. We are not ready to go out into the world until we have quit being of the world.

There will be no revival until the church repents. There is God's side: "It is time for thee, Lord, to work: for they have made void thy law" (Psalms 119:126). There is man's side: "Sow to yourselves in righteousness, reap in mercy; break up your fallow ground: it is time to seek the Lord, till he come and rain righteousness upon you" (Hosea 10:12). "It is time for thee, Lord, to work." That is God's business. "It is time to seek the Lord." That is our business. We must break up the fallow ground. Fallow ground is unproductive because it is undisturbed. Can we have a revival in depth in a shallow generation? A pastor was asked, "How large is your parish?" And he replied, "It is twenty miles wide and one inch deep!"

This generation has never seen a great revival like the English and American Revivals, the Welsh Revival, the Shantung Revival. We do not know what revival is. We confuse it with evangelism.

Evangelism is the proclamation of the gospel to win the lost. Revival is a work of the Spirit of God among Christians. We do not want revival. Dr. R. A. Torrey said that if most church members understood what revival really means they would pray, "Lord, keep us from having a revival!" Most church members today would vote against a revival, and indeed they do, for most of them never come to church when an effort is made to have revival. We do not feel that we need a revival. Laodicea was rich and prosperous and had need of nothing. We forget that the goodness of God in our prosperity should lead us to repentance. We will not pay the price of revival: confession of sin—private, personal, and public; restitution—as in the case of Zacchaeus (if some church members were converted they'd wear out sole leather carrying back things that don't belong to them!); renunciation—the forsaking as well as confession of sin. We settle for less than revival; we settle for church meetings "as usual" that never get to the root of the matter in brokenness before God with humble and contrite hearts.

We know too much. We decide what kind of revival we want and we ask God to sign on our little dotted line. God is not signing on anybody's dotted line. We must bow to the sovereignty of the Holy Spirit.

I heard of two men who stood in front of a taxidermist's window and criticized his work. "Look at that bird over there," one said. "Nobody ever saw a bird sit on a limb like that." Just then the bird flew down! We decide how God should do it and then the bird flies down! If revival ever comes, some experts will be embarrassed!

> Come, Holy Spirit, heavenly Dove
> With all thy quickening powers!
> Kindle a flame of sacred love
> In these cold hearts of ours.

It is time for the heavenly Dove to fly down!
J. B. Phillips says the church is so rich she is fat and out of

breath and so organized that she is musclebound. *Out of breath!*
God breathed into Adam the breath of life. Our Lord breathed
on his disciples and said, "Receive ye the Holy Ghost."The church
is trying to exhale all the time without inhaling. We must breathe
*into* us what God breathes *upon* us.

When I was a boy, my father used to take me to an old-fashioned mill by a stream whose waters flowed onto the big water
wheel that turned all the other wheels in the mill. If the creek
became clogged or diverted so there was not enough water to
operate the mill, the miller didn't attempt to turn the wheel by
hand; he just went up creek and cleared the channel, by removing
whatever was blocking the water's flow.

Yet, all over the land I find pastors, educational directors,
music leaders, Sunday school superintendents straining and
striving to make our church wheels go around. We need to "go
up the creek," get sin out of our hearts and lives, remove the hin-
drances and debris. Then the Spirit would flow, the wheels would
turn, and we would have something to show for our grinding.
After all, the secret of the Acts of the Apostles was the inflow,
the outflow, and the overflow of the Holy Spirit. Are you ready
to "go up the creek" and make way for that inflow in your heart
and home and church?

We shall not need to worry about the outflow if there is a
powerful inflow. A mighty stream flowing into a lake will find
a way out and make a channel of its own. Dr. Phillips says the
early church was "open on the Godward side." Any Christian or
church open to the Spirit's inflow will overflow on the manward
side. We are always driving and striving to get the laymen out,
to evangelize, to witness, to communicate, to get the gospel to
the world. Religious engineers are digging new channels for the
outflow but an Acts-of-the-Apostles inflow of the Spirit would
sweep over all our little arrangements, inundate the community, and flood the world around. The great revivals of the past
upset all of the calculations of the experts. The rushing stream
of divine power made its own channels. Some of them were
unusual and unconventional and not at all according to plans

and specifications in the blueprints of ecclesiastical engineers. The Welsh Revival, for instance, broke over all the dykes and overflowed all the regular river banks. Any Christian or church open to God without obstruction will need no pep meetings, promotional drives, and kickoff suppers to become a torrent of blessing. From within rivers of living water shall flow. Our Lord made it perfectly plain that if we come and drink we shall be springs of water welling up into eternal life. But, as the song puts it, we cannot be channels of blessing if our lives are not free from known sin; so the problem is to "go up the creek" and open our lives on the Godward side. The church must first repent.

There are those who say that revivals don't last. Of course they don't. They are not supposed to last. Childhood doesn't last. Springtime doesn't last. Courtship doesn't last. Revival gets the church up from subnormal to normal, then the church carries on upon a new level. The fruits and benefits of revival last, but the revival as the instrument of renewal passes. Sometimes when we are subnormal physically, surgery is required. When health is restored we do not stay in the hospital. Great emergencies like flood and fire require emergency measures, and all normal schedules are disrupted; but when normalcy is restored, the crisis measures are no longer employed. In true revival, high emotional fervor, all-night prayer-meetings, extraordinary experiences are in order; pleasure haunts are forsaken, ordinary interests are forgotten, the forces of evil are aroused in bitter hostility. Some of these features could not continue indefinitely; but once the purpose of revival is achieved and the church purified, things proceed on a more even pitch but on a higher level than before. Revival is super-normal – it pulls the subnormal church up to normal, but it must not be confused with the abnormal, which is found when even good things are carried to excess. Revival is a means to an end, and when the end is obtained the means has served its purpose and does not continue indefinitely. Pentecost lasted only a day. Revivals serve their generation by the will of God. They swing the church from one extreme to the other, then back to normal.

Evan Roberts, so used of God in the Welsh Revival, warned that the fever heat could not be kept going long but that the church could be raised to a higher level, then settle down. We are not to build three tabernacles on the "Mount of Revival," but to bring the glory down the mountain into everyday living and service.

Whether or not the church will repent today I know not, but revival is the top item on God's agenda, and there is no use talking about anything else until we attend to that. We cannot move on to number two or number three until we have done something about number one. If a sick man needs surgery, the doctor would be a criminal if he said, "I don't want to make you uncomfortable and force you to disrupt your customary schedule, so we will dispense with radical surgery. Just get out in the sunshine, change your outlook, and get busy." Today, something like that often is prescribed for sick churches that need revival. Soothing syrup is no substitute for surgery. Whether or not in this nuclear space age people will listen to this kind of preaching anymore remains to be seen, but one thing is certain: if we will not repent, there is nothing left but judgment. If Laodicea will not be zealous and repent, the Lord will spew her out of his mouth. Nothing else is enough.

The church must first repent.

# CHAPTER 18

# "Go To Jesus"

A good friend of mine, now with the Lord, used to offer a simple little formula for everything: "Go to Jesus." He held that amidst all the perplexities of life—the differences among theologians, problems of Bible interpretation—if we get tangled up we can always go directly to Jesus himself. Not only is it gloriously true that we need no middleman, no earthly priest, through whom we may reach God for salvation, but it is also wonderfully true that we can go to our Lord himself for everything else, great or small. Like the poor sick woman who pressed through the crowd and reached him for herself, we can push through any multitude today and touch the hem of his garment.

Alas, even Bible scholars sometimes hinder more than they help. I have read books about guidance, healing, assurance, and power that confused more than they clarified. I had to lay all that aside and come firsthand to the Lord for myself. Some books that figure out everything in convenient heads and subheads leave me cold. Jesus Christ transcends all our definitions. We cannot pour the truth about him into our little mental receptacles—so much runs over.

> Our little systems have their day;
> They have their day and cease to be;
> They are but broken gleams of thee,
> And thou, O Lord, art more than they.

There are times when one grows weary of all he has read and heard and feels like the man who wished he had never read the Gospel of John so that he could read it for the first time! It is a blessed thing that we do not have to clear everything with the theologians before we can go to Jesus. He is always available and accessible, and some who have proved him best have been plain souls who took the shortcut and came directly for themselves.

Those who came to him in the days of his flesh had not listened to Bible scholars arguing "about it and about." Our Lord healed three blind men in three distinctly different ways and three schools of thought might easily have started right there: the One-Touch School, the Two-Touch School, and the Go-Wash-in-Siloam School. What matters is that all three got to Jesus; all three who once were blind could say, "Now I see."

The Savior is not walking around visibly as he did in Galilee but "more blessed are they that have not seen and yet have believed." Anybody can get to Jesus anytime, anywhere. I have often wondered what would happen if somebody would really set out just to trust him *for everything*. Why not? Life's threads are pitifully tangled these days, and only he can straighten them out. We do our best when we go to him. And remember, anything short of that is utter failure, no matter how conscientiously we try to unravel the threads. His office is always open. You do not have to wait. He is only a prayer away.

# CHAPTER 19

# Doing It the Little Way

I am going to take a position that may not win many friends or influence many people, but it is scriptural and deserves our consideration. We live in a day when size is the criterion—whatever the sort may be. Everything must be done the big way. This is true in the church as in the world. We think and plan in terms of the huge, the colossal, the super-duper. Big churches, great crowds, impressive statistics... one would think God never condescends to visit fewer than a thousand people. Oh, I know we quote the verse about "Where two or three are gathered in my name," but we use it to comfort ourselves on a poor prayer-meeting night when we are more conscious of the absence of the people than of the presence of the Lord. We forget that while our Lord preached to multitudes (and preached them away!), he did his greatest work with a few. We say little of the fact that some of the greatest events in church history from Pentecost on did not require a multitude. We are thinking big these days; and with moon trips in prospect and the national debt in billions, the church has caught the spirit of the times. We have been doing it the big way, but in the midst of our fabulous planning and programming we hear the lament of worried churchmen. The mountain labors and brings forth a mouse. With the biggest set-up in history we have least to show for it. Maybe we ought to try doing it the little way.

Consider Gideon. The Midianites were "as grasshoppers for multitude..." (Judges 6:5). They were out to do it the big way. Gideon started out with pretty much the same idea. He had thirty-two thousand men, which is not a large army, but for Gideon and his times it was considerable. But God, who is not always

on the side of the strongest battalions, said, "The people that
are with thee are too many for me to give the Midianites into
their hands." The reason was forthcoming: "Lest Israel vaunt
themselves against me, saying, Mine own hand hath saved me"
(Judges 7:2). In other words, "If you do it the big way, Israel and
not God will get the glory."

Gideon was out to fight a peculiar kind of warfare and to
win a peculiar kind of victory. If this had been ordinary conflict,
the usual preparation would have been in order. He would have
needed more men, not fewer. But this was God's battle and it was
to be fought God's way. Gideon had too many soldiers for the
kind of victory he was out to win.

The church is engaged in a peculiar conflict. We are not con-
tending with flesh and blood but with "the power that controls
this dark world and spiritual agents of the very headquarters
of evil." This is not conventional warfare, and the fight is with
spiritual, not carnal, weapons. Most church people do not have
the slightest understanding of the true nature of Christian warfare. We are fighting the greatest battle of all time with the most
unprepared army on earth. The battle is Christ against antichrist,
and in no way, shape, or form is it to be compared to any human-
itarian project, political program, or social reform. Somehow we
have gotten the idea that we can fight on conventional lines by
ordinary human know-how. We are trying to do it the big way;
but if we won the battle that way, just as in Gideon's day, we
would take the credit and God would get no glory. But we are
not winning it; and God is not going to let us win it this way, for
it is his battle, not ours.

Just as with Gideon, so with the church. We have too many
soldiers of the kind we have for the kind of battle we are in.
Most of our church people are totally unprepared, untrained,
and unequipped for spiritual warfare. Of course, no swivel-chair
general would dream of reducing our army from thirty-two
thousand to three hundred. He would insist on increasing it to a
hundred thousand! But God's ways are not our ways. The average church member thinks the work of the church is not too

different from any other enterprise except that it is done under religious auspices. Therefore we assume that if we have enough people and enough money and fight hard enough we can win the battle. But we are equipping David with Saul's armor, when God would defeat Goliath by sling and stone. Most of our army has to be conscripted and may desert on the slightest provocation. The victory God is out to win is not won by a mob but by a miracle, and we are not operating on a miraculous basis these days. Gideon won with a handful of soldiers armed with lamps and pitchers. Whoever heard of such strategy? It violates all rules of conventional warfare. We have mobilized instead of mobilized. We do not need a host outfitted from the arsenals of earth, but a handful armed on Paul's pattern in Ephesians. We cannot win a spiritual battle with carnal weapons. We cannot gain a heavenly victory with a worldly army.

God thinned out Gideon's host by dividing it into three classifications. Dr. Graham Scroggie called them "Those Who Dread, Those Who Delay, Those Who Dare." God sent home twenty-two thousand cowards, "fearful and afraid." The proportion would be about the same today. Most church members are afraid to stand up and be counted. A Sunday morning congregation is impressive to look at; but, for the kind of battle we have on our hands today, most of them are disqualified. They make good soldiers in a dress parade when the flags are waving and the bugles are blowing; but if they are shot in battle it will be in the back, for they are cowards on moral and spiritual issues. In an age of moral fogs and spiritual twilights, when black and white have merged into gray, they are conformists who dare not challenge the pattern of the community, middle-of-the-roaders, afraid of being called queer and old-fashioned and out of step with progress. The battle of the Lord is no place for a coward with a cotton string for a backbone.

After the cowards came ninety-seven hundred who were careless—on all fours—at the mercy of the enemy. Another big portion of our church people is disqualified for spiritual warfare because they are not alert but off guard with their defenses down, thinking more of satisfying their own desires than of enduring hardness as good soldiers of Jesus Christ. The Lord's battle is no place for the careless. It demands that we walk circumspectly, that we be sober and vigilant, that we watch and pray, that we be not deceived. We are up against the most subtle adversary of all, and it is no time to be on all fours drinking from every brook that flows by.

There remained three hundred competent and committed, who cupped the water in their hands, more interested in being ready to fight than in satisfying their thirst. They were in dead earnest; their minds were on the battle; they were out to win a victory and water was incidental.

Encompassed as we are today by the enemy, we will not win the battle with a multitude of the cowards and the careless, but with a dedicated minority of the committed. We have been trying to fight the big way. Maybe we ought to try the little way. I do not mean that we must discharge all the cowards and dismiss all the careless. We need to reclaim all we can and try to make good soldiers of them. Indeed we read that when Gideon's band won the battle, multitudes of others, including no doubt these delinquents, joined them in pursuing the enemy! What we are saying is that the kind of battle we are out to fight and the kind of victory we are out to win calls for a Gideon's band, not a motley mob. We must recruit in our churches a Master's minority, a company of the committed, a faithful few, the church within the church, a spearhead of dependables and expendables who know what spiritual warfare is and who wear the whole armor of God. We do not have many of this kind. Too many confuse the fight of faith with a few hours of church work, church attendance on Sunday, and a little money in a duplex envelope. It includes that, but the Lord's battle goes on night and day, seven days a week. It is open only to volunteers and nobody is retired on a pension. It is fought at home, in the shop and office, on the campus, at work or play, whether young or old, sick or well, rich or poor. We gather at church for instruction and training, but the battle goes on everywhere.

If we are to win this fight we must understand what kind of warfare it is. It is God's battle against an unseen foe. It is not a Baptist or a Methodist or a Protestant or a fundamentalist battle—"the battle is the Lord's." We must not underestimate our adversary.

Teddy Roosevelt had a dog that often was badly beaten in a fight. Once, after the poor pooch had taken an unmerciful licking from a mangy cur, a friend of Roosevelt's said to the colonel, "Your dog isn't much of a fighter." Teddy replied, "Oh, he's a good fighter but he's a poor judge of dogs!"

We must not be ignorant of Satan's devices or underrate our foe. But neither must we underestimate our ally. When the Syrian army surrounded Elisha the grand old prophet encouraged his terrified servant by saying, "Fear not; for they that are with us are more than they that are with them" (2 Kings 6:16).

We have thought, "If we had more members, more money, a better program, we could prevail." We need to recruit a band of Christian commandos who love not their lives unto death, but who believe there is no substitute for victory—who are out to win. We need the spirit of the captain who cried to his little band encompassed by the enemy: "Men, we are surrounded... don't let one of them escape!"

We have tried it the big way. Let us try it the little way. We have tried it the extensive way. Let us try the intensive way. A pastor said recently, "My pastorate is twenty miles wide and one inch deep!" We have gone all out on width; we had better do something about the depth of our enterprise. Shallowness and superficiality abound. It is time for the intensive training of a Gideon's band in every church, who will make up in sort for what they lack in size, the church within the church, fighting God's battle God's way.

CHAPTER 20

# Beware of the Bypass!

The prophet Jeremiah exhorts us: "Stand ye in the ways, and see, and ask for the old paths, where is the good way, and walk therein, and ye shall find rest for your souls" (Jeremiah 6:16). Peter writes of those "who have forsaken the right way and are gone astray."

This is the day of the bypass. Great freeways skirt the edges of town after town, detour here and circumvent there. In this madhouse of traffic congestion when we are safer on a battle-field than on a highway, the bypass is a necessity. But there are some bypasses that belong to another category. There is a King's Highway from earth to heaven, and all along its course the devil has built a clever system of detours. "The way of the cross leads home," but there is another way "that seemeth right unto a man." It bypasses the old familiar landmarks and "the end thereof are the ways of death." The detour is always rougher than the main road.

*We are bypassing sin.* We have given it new names: imma-turity, arrested development, biological growing pains. We call weakness what God calls wickedness. We are sick but not sinful. Alcoholism is only a disease (the only one I know of on which we spend millions of dollars a year to spread!). A liar is only an extrovert with a lively imagination. Adultery is not a sin in Hol-lywood. A murderer is only a victim of a traumatic experience. Illegitimacy is now respectable and is subsidized by the welfare state.

The book of Romans begins with a fearful delineation of sin, the depravity of the human heart and race. Paul Bunyan says that when God starts to tune an instrument he begins with the base.

We cannot ignore sin and get away with it. We used to believe that people were "lost" and needed to be "saved." How many parents now believe their children are "lost" without Christ? "But Johnny is a good boy." So was the rich young ruler, but he went away from Jesus. We are not calling sinners to repentance these days, we are calling the righteous—and not even to repentance, for we have made Christianity so mild that men can come into the church just as they are and never know any difference.

We are calling people to dedication that leaves sin untouched. We would have Isaiah say "Here am I," before he has ever said, "Woe is me!" We would tell sick men simply to go out and act like well men, overlooking their disease.

> You cannot be a channel of blessing
> If your life is not free from known sin.

The church is bypassing sin. After Israel was defeated at Ai, Joshua might have said, "We have suffered a little setback; but let us regroup, throw our shoulders back, and try again." But God said, "*Israel* hath sinned." The sin of the individual affects the whole group. Today we would advise Paul not to deal with the incestuous man or any other church troubles in Corinth lest it "tear up the church." We would have him "accentuate the positive" but, as G. Campbell Morgan has pointed out, Paul began with the "carnalities" and then moved on to the "spiritualities." A church business meeting in Pergamos these days would not dare touch Balaamism—"Better get along with the Balaamites and let well enough alone." And who would dream of stirring up Jezebel in Thyatira? So we "close ranks" and go ahead ignoring sin in the church, forgetting that "a little leaven leaveneth the whole lump." One bad apple can spoil a barrel of good apples. We try to sweep out the cobwebs without touching the spider. We mop the floor but leave the faucet running. We try to control the weeds but disregard the seeds from which the weeds grow. Sin cannot be bypassed. There must be confession and cleansing.

In the second place, *we are bypassing the cross.* The devil hates the cross and, ever since Jesus came, the strategy of Satan has been to detour around Calvary. In the third temptation he offered the kingdoms of this world to the Savior, but our Lord would not take a shortcut. He would go the way of the cross and get the kingdoms of the world as promised by his Father.

Peter confessed the Christ but denied the cross. He acknowledged the Son of God but sought to divert him from the way of Calvary. "This shall not be unto thee." Today men preach Christ the teacher, the example; Christ the paragon but not Christ the propitiation; the crystal Christ but not the Calvary Christ. Oh, they make him out to be a Martyr, but not the Son of God with no sin in him but all sin on him, dying for all the sins of all the world.

Our Lord said to Peter, "Get thee behind me, Satan." There is something diabolic about the denial of the cross, and our Savior would have none of it though it came from the lips of Peter himself.

Today science would circumvent Calvary and seek to accomplish by artificial and even chemical devices that which comes only by the cross. A popular magazine recently carried this statement: "LSD has been shown through carefully controlled experiments to be the key to a scientific understanding of man's religious and mystical experiences." Man would produce today by drugs an experience of God that comes only by way of Calvary.

Even Christians would give the cross the runaround. They go through the ordinance of baptism but deny in their lives that identification with Christ in death and resurrection which baptism symbolizes. They know nothing of death to sin, to self, to the world. They do not walk in newness of life.

Our Lord faced the baptism of death (Luke 12:50). He said to James and John: "I have a baptism to be baptized with." Our great church bodies today want grandstand seats in glory as did James and John, but they are not interested in the shame and reproach of the old rugged cross.

Paul said, "I am crucified with Christ" (Galatians 2:20). He did not bypass the cross. It was the heart of his experience, "an *I* crossed out," and he preached Christ *crucified*. He spoke of "enemies of the cross" who would bypass Calvary. Our Lord made it central: "And I, if I be lifted up from the earth, will draw all men unto me" (John 12:32). There is no power in a life or message that detours around the cross. "The way of the cross leads home"; and all bypasses, all detours, all shortcuts lead to destruction.

Finally, *we are bypassing the Lord's return*. Of course we can't ignore it altogether. Any doctrine as prominent in the New Testament as this cannot be disregarded completely. Years ago Dr. Hinson of Portland preached a great sermon one Sunday on the Second Coming. Some students spoke to him after the service and one said, "We just can't get this out of the New Testament the way you preached it today." "Of course not," replied the great preacher, "it's in there to stay!"

This precious truth is the unwanted stepchild in the family of church doctrine. It was said of A. J. Gordon concerning this blessed hope, "Advocacy of this doctrine cost him much. It seems to awaken suspicion and lead to estrangement, this great doctrine of hope. He used to say, 'It is not wanted by a church with millionaire merchants and by the great universities. But, after all, it was for the assertion of this doctrine that our Lord was crucified!'"

We pay it the tribute of our lips, but it is very evident that it does not thrill many of us, nor do we love his appearing and look for him with glad anticipation. Some say that all we can do is to be ready, but the New Testament Christians were not only ready, they were expectant. G. Campbell Morgan used to say that he never laid his head on the pillow at night without thinking, "Before the morning comes the final morning may have come!"

We bypass the Lord's return because the belief that he may come at any time, and that God is not converting the world but taking out a people for his name, does not fit our grandiose plans for building the kingdom of heaven on earth. We politely soft-pedal it as being controversial, but any doctrine of the

Christian faith is controversial. One would think the blessed hope would be on the lips of every Christian, that we would greet each other with "Maranatha!" but instead we look embarrassed and change the subject when somebody brings it up. And because we have given it the silent treatment, our perspective is warped and our vision is blurred; and while God is out to do one thing we are doing something else. If we do not know where we are going we shall not know what to do nor how to do it where we are. It is about time we got around to God's program, not of Christianizing society but of evangelizing the world, taking out a remnant from a doomed civilization.

It is the day of the bypass. It will be a great day for the church when we get off our detours and onto the King's Highway!

To obtain additional copies of this book, and to see a list of
other great Christian titles, visit our web site:
www.KingsleyPress.com